CW00968543

BRAMBLY HEDGE
COLLECTORS BOOK

Louise Irvine

RICHARD
DENNIS

ACKNOWLEDGEMENTS

This book would not have been possible without the talents of Jill Barklem who created the mice of Brambly Hedge and I am grateful for all Jill's kindness and hospitality when we met to talk about her life and work. Her literary agent, Laura Cecil, has also been very helpful, arranging photographs and reviewing the text.

I have followed the development of Brambly Hedge character merchandise since the early 1980s when I worked for Royal Doulton and I was delighted when Richard Dennis asked me to write the first collectors book on the subject. He first recognised the need for such a book several years ago and his continuing commitment and enthusiasm have made it a reality.

I am also indebted to the staff of Copyrights, notably Linda Pooley, Karen Addison and Julie Tustian, who provided so much information about the companies they license to produce Brambly Hedge designs. The companies involved have also been most helpful and I should like to thank the following individuals: Elizabeth Bart-Smith of Border Fine Arts; Marilyn Rocca of Crummles; Jane Hill of Enesco; Frances Wilson of Hantel; Ray Dowding and Sue Reed of Lakeland Studios; Terry Selman and Julie Tilstone of Lawleys by Post; Paula Pointon, Julie McKeown and Valerie Baynton of Royal Doulton. Keith Pybus and Roger Miller also provided helpful reminiscences about the development of Brambly Hedge at Royal Doulton. The modellers and designers, who interpreted Jill Barklem's illustrations for new media, have provided much information and original artwork for the book and I am especially grateful to Peter Roberts, Harry Sales and Richard Wawrzesta.

Thanks also to the collectors who have contributed, especially Emma Munford who made her extensive collection available for photography and study, Jo Ann Travis of the USA and Birgit Grunwald of Europe. Several specialist dealers and retailers have also assisted me with information and photographs, notably Adam Lovejoy of When We Were Young, Nick Tzimas of UK International Ceramics, Bob Smith of Cameron and Smith, and Bruce Wheeler from Wheelers of Loughborough.

The design and production teams at Richard Dennis and Flaydemouse have also been very patient and understanding as the book has evolved, especially Wendy Wort, Sue Evans, Chrissie Bursey and Magnus Dennis.

Finally, I should like to thank my husband, George, and son, Ben, for their constant support and encouragement.

Production Wendy Wort

Photography by Magnus Dennis

Print, design and reproduction by Flaydemouse, Yeovil, Somerset

Published by Richard Dennis, The Old Chapel, Shepton Beauchamp, Somerset TA19 OLE

© 1999 Brambly Hedge, Jill Barklem

© 1999 Richard Dennis & Louise Irvine

ISBN 0 903685 65 5 Softback   ISBN 0 903685 75 2 Hardback

All rights reserved

British Library Cataloguing-in-Publication Data. A catalogue record for this book is available from the British Library

This book is an independent publication and neither the author nor the publisher has any connection with the companies here mentioned. Any opinions expressed are entirely the personal views of the author. The names of the companies featured in this book are all registered trade marks and are used herein to express items of collector interest. The copyright, in each instance, belongs to the individual manufacturers.

CONTENTS

FOREWORD
BY JILL BARKLEM

People sometimes say to me what a lovely way to spend your time – writing and illustrating children's books. Well, I suppose it is, in a way, but it is also jolly HARD! I have lovely pictures in my head – the problem is getting them onto paper.

I will sometimes do thirty or forty rough drawings to try to catch what I see, and get the three dimensions of the real world into a two-dimensional medium. When Royal Doulton turned my two-dimensional world back into three-dimensional reality, it was so exciting to see the real rounded models of mice taking shape. When they were finally coloured and fired, you could hold them in your hand, and play with them (if you were very careful!).

I first thought of Brambly Hedge on the train, travelling to art school in London. I watched the banks, fields and hedges as they passed, and tried to imagine what was going on in the passing hedgerows. My interest in the country, and country ways, led me to envisage an idyllic country life, completely reliant on the natural resources around – in fact much as our distant ancestors must have lived – but in miniature, dolls house-sized proportions. I became fascinated by the whole concept, and started to draw pictures and research relevant details. Finally I took the ideas to Collins Publishers. My editor, Jane Fior, instantly saw what I was trying to do, and has been in immense help and inspiration ever since.

So, the books were produced and published in 1980. I was lucky enough to get coverage in the *Sunday Times* colour supplement. This was seen by Keith Pybus, Marketing Director of Doulton, who saw potential for a range of ceramics. A meeting was arranged with Harry Sales and Peter Roberts, Design Managers at Doulton. They were very enthusiastic, and caring, and I somehow knew my mice would be safe in their hands...

THE STORY OF
BRAMBLY HEDGE

'It was the most beautiful morning. The spring sunshine crept into every cottage along Brambly Hedge, and the little windows in the trees were opened wide. All the mice were up early, but earliest of all was Wilfred, who lived with his family in the hornbeam tree. It was Wilfred's birthday.'

Cover of *Spring Story*.

Illustration showing the mice of Brambly Hedge.

So begins Jill Barklem's series of books about the everyday lives of wood mice living in the English hedgerow. The *Spring, Summer, Autumn* and *Winter* stories were published in 1980 to immediate acclaim and, before long, various manufacturers were requesting licences to reproduce her characters in other media. Jill no longer had time to illustrate other people's books and began to concentrate fully on Brambly Hedge. Little did she dream in the early 1970s that her travel doodles would lead to such a successful business.

It was the monotony of Jill's daily train journey from Epping to art school in central London that prompted her fantasies about a self-sufficient community of mice living in the hedgerows that she passed by. Throughout the changing seasons, she filled notebooks with ideas and sketches and in the evenings she began to collect information about rural life in pre-industrial England. For a while Jill kept mice as models and she studied their different mannerisms and features down to the last whisker before adding the fashions of yesteryear. Initially, she did not envisage publishing her private dream-world but in 1978 her new husband, David, persuaded her to share her vision with others and Collins signed her up after seeing two panoramas of mouse life and her notes on the subject.

*Haffertee Goes
Exploring,*
a book illustrated
by Jill.

Jill spent many months composing her stories and refining her drawings for publication. She works in a meticulous fashion, producing dozens of rough sketches before arriving at a satisfactory composition, and each full-page illustration will take two or three months to complete. Jill learned to draw as a child after suffering a detached retina. As sports were not recommended for her condition, she spent hours in the school art room drawing from nature. Jill believes that determination and good powers of observation are the essential requirements of a successful artist and she perfected her own personal style by intensive study of the world about her.

The menu for the Brambly Hedge
luncheon, hosted by Royal Doulton.

Reading was another of Jill's great pleasures and her childhood favourites included the *Milly Molly Mandy* stories, *The Little Grey Rabbit* books by Alison Uttley and anything written by Enid Blyton. At the age of eight, Jill sent her story about *Pinky the Fairy* to Miss Blyton and received a postcard recommending that she improve her language and punctuation skills in English classes. Jill took the advice to heart and spent her school years studying hard. At one time, she considered reading zoology at university, but her interest in art triumphed and she attended St Martin's School of Art in central London to study illustration. When she graduated in 1974, she began to illustrate children's books under her maiden name, Gillian Gaze, and these included a series of stories about *Haffertee the Hamster* by Janet and John Perkins. There are hints of Brambly Hedge in some of her early work but it was the totality of Jill's own mouse world that captivated adults and children alike. She has received letters from elderly ladies who appreciate the nostalgic qualities of life in Brambly Hedge and she has had correspondence with engineers and craftsmen, praising the authenticity of her designs.

Jill spent many years researching the lifestyles of the Brambly Hedge mice and amassed piles of fascinating memoranda, including some lovely old sepia photographs of country folk with smocks, straw hats and hobnailed boots. She studied traditional tools and crafts and once she even constructed a mouse-size water wheel to test the efficiency of her design. She also collects old kitchen crockery, including pieces of blue and white spotted Dartmouth pottery and striped Cornish ware, examples of which appear in her Brambly Hedge drawings. Other things that cry out to Jill 'take me home' include wooden spoons that have been worn down with years of baking and well-used enamel jugs with chips and dents. Although her own kitchen was only built on to her house in 1997, it has the warm lived-in look of an old country farmhouse created by kitchen cupboards with cleverly distressed paint-work. Her husband used to deal in antiques and reconditioned pine furniture and these were put to good use in many of the Brambly Hedge interiors. Together, they have created a kitchen worthy of Mrs Apple, the most accomplished cook in Brambly Hedge.

Apparently Mrs Apple was based on Jill's grandmother and she has fond memories of sitting at her table as a child, waiting to lick the bowl of cake mix. She has inherited her grandmother's expertise in the kitchen and she loves to conserve, dry and pickle seasonal fare,

just like the mice in Brambly Hedge. The pages of her old recipe books are well-thumbed after years of experimenting with delicious dishes to share with her mouse friends. In the course of her research, Jill's family and friends have dined on nettle soup, hazelnut roulade and chestnut pie amongst other delicacies.

Jill's grandfather was a gardener in a big house and she acknowledges his influence in her great love of nature. She prowls around her beloved garden observing the wildlife and looking for interesting details to add to her books. On her rambles through Epping Forest, she takes photographs of gnarled old tree trunks or tangled bramble bushes at various times of the year and she picks through the undergrowth collecting twigs, seeds, mushrooms, feathers

Jill Barklem's desk.

Jill's kitchen.

Jill's pottery collection.

Emma Munford with her Royal Doulton collection.

Emma's twenty-first birthday cake made by her mother.

and flowers. The most interesting specimens are retained in the cubby holes of her desk where she can study them at leisure. Although she has moved house several times, her desk is always lovingly arranged in exactly the same way so that she can recreate the atmosphere of Brambly Hedge with ease.

The fascinating background to the Brambly Hedge stories was first reported in the *Sunday Times Supplement* in September 1980 to coincide with the launch of the first books, and this article caught the attention of Royal Doulton's marketing director, Keith Pybus, and his brand manager, Simon Bell. They had been looking around for new imagery to extend their giftware range and they believed that Brambly Hedge would be perfect for interpretation in ceramic. An approach was made to Collins the publishers and the enquiry was handled by Linda Pooley, one of the managers of children's books. Linda also understood the potential of the Brambly Hedge mice and when she left Collins to work for Copyrights, the merchandise agents for writers and artists, she was asked to represent Jill Barklem's interests.

The new Copyrights company aimed to develop the merchandising of children's characters beyond the basic plastic beakers that prevailed in the 1970s. The managing director, Nicholas Durbridge, had worked on the first licensed contracts for *Paddington Bear,* who appeared on a wide variety of products, and he offered a similar service for other successful properties. Royal Doulton were granted the licence to reproduce Brambly Hedge characters as earthenware figures and on bone china giftware. Their designers, Harry Sales and Peter Roberts, worked very closely with Copyrights and Jill Barklem to develop the first Brambly Hedge collection, which was launched in 1983.

Meanwhile, manufacturers of stationery, greetings cards, cosmetics and soft toys also appreciated how effectively Brambly Hedge could sell their products as gift buyers around the world succumbed to the charms of these magical mice. In 1983, Crummles were granted a licence to reproduce scenes from Brambly Hedge on fine enamel boxes and in 1987

Border Fine Arts, together with the American company Enesco, secured the rights to recreate the leading characters as resin figures. More recently, Hantel Victorian Miniatures have launched pewter figures and the Wedgwood factory has produced a series of decorative china plates. These prestigious companies each have a keen collector following and gradually the Brambly Hedge mice have been promoted from casual gifts to compulsive collectables.

Emma Munford, whose collection forms the basis of this book, began collecting Brambly Hedge when she was a child and, over the years, she has found virtually all the pieces made by Royal Doulton, Border Fine Arts, Enesco, Crummles and Hantel as well as samples of stationery, textiles and toys. Not all Brambly Hedge fans seek out as many different brands as Emma but there are specialist collectors all over the globe and the activities of the Brambly Hedge mice in the marketplace are avidly discussed on the worldwide web. The Brambly Hedge books have now been translated into fifteen languages from Finnish to Korean and there is so much enthusiasm for the celebrated

mice in Japan that the Hankyu department store has dedicated its Christmas windows to Jill Barklem's tales for the last six years.

Jill followed the success of the first four Brambly Hedge stories with the *The Secret Staircase* in 1983, which was developed from a bedtime story about the adventures of Wilfred and Primrose told to her young daughter, Elizabeth. The exploits of Wilfred Toadflax continued in her next book *The High Hills* (1986) which was dedicated to her son, Peter, who identified with this mischievous little mouse. A few years later came *Sea Story* (1990) prompted by the Barklem's new holiday cottage on the Suffolk coast. This nautical tale gave a new dimension to the mouse experience with sand and sea replacing forest and hedgerows. The new stories prompted many more letters from readers around the world and Jill has always endeavoured to write back personally, particularly to young children. She has never forgotten how much she valued her postcard from Enid Blyton. One question cropped up in her correspondence with increasing regularity – will Poppy and Dusty ever have a family?

Jill Barklem with Linda Pooley and David Barklem.

Fourteen years after their wedding in *Summer Story*, the long-awaited event took place in *Poppy's Babies* which was published in 1994.

Fans around the world are now looking forward to another title but Jill has been busy during the last few years working with the producers of the animated Brambly Hedge films. She had to provide new artwork for the models that appeared in the stop-frame animations as well as approve all the visual effects created by Cosgrove Hall and Hot Animation. Over seven million viewers watched the *Winter Story* on BBC television on Christmas Day 1996 and, since then, most of Jill's other stories have been filmed and are attracting new fans through television programmes as far afield as Australia and Mexico. The Brambly Hedge mice are now international movie stars and the success of their films has given more scope to designers of licensed products. Copyrights, together with Jill and David Barklem, are now very busy preparing for the twentieth anniversary of Brambly Hedge in the year 2000, so look out for more news of these very special mice in the new millennium.

Illustration from *Poppy's Babies*.

WHO'S WHO IN
BRAMBLY HEDGE

BASIL

With his sensitive nose for fine wine, Basil is in charge of all the cellars under the Store Stump. He has long white whiskers and wears a scarlet waistcoat. In the *Summer Story*, he selects the wines for the wedding party and he makes hot blackberry punch in the *Winter Story*.

CATKIN

One of the Toadflax children, Catkin is chased around the kitchen by her brothers with pawfuls of snow in the *Winter Story*. Later in the story they put icicles down her dress.

CLOVER

One of the Toadflax children, Clover makes toast by the fire in the *Winter Story* and she helps string crab apples to roast. At the Snow Ball she dances with her brothers but they whirl her round so fast that she does not feel very well.

CONKER

Dusty's friend, Conker, is the best man at the wedding ceremony in the *Summer Story*. Together they get covered in flour dust before the great occasion.

DUSTY DOGWOOD

Dusty Dogwood is the miller and was given his name because he is always covered in flour dust. He marries Poppy Eyebright in the *Summer Story* and later appears with his family in the story of *Poppy's Babies*.

FLAX WEAVER

In *The High Hills*, Flax Weaver and his wife Lily make blankets for the voles.

LADY WOODMOUSE

Old Oak Palace, which is featured in the *Spring Story* and *The Secret Staircase*, is the home of the Woodmouse family. Daisy, Lady Woodmouse is also one of the main characters in the *Autumn Story*.

LILY WEAVER

Lily is Flax Weaver's wife and she helps him replace the voles' moth-eaten blankets. She does the spinning whilst her husband does the weaving.

LORD WOODMOUSE

Lord Woodmouse is the head of Brambly Hedge and his family has always lived at the Old Oak Palace. He presides over all the celebrations in the community and is one of the main characters in the *Autumn Story* when his daughter Primrose is lost in the woods.

MR APPLE

In the *Spring Story*, Mr Apple is introduced as warden of The Store Stump. He is also the father of Daisy, Lady Woodmouse. In the *Winter Story*, he announces the Snow Ball.

MRS APPLE

A wonderful cook, Mrs Apple lives with her husband at Crabapple Cottage and appears with delicious food in all the Four Seasons tales. She is always ready to lend a helping hand to her daughter, Lady Woodmouse.

MRS CRUSTYBREAD

As the cook at Old Oak Palace, Mrs Crustybread is kept busy with her rolling pin. She makes Wilfred a birthday cake in the *Spring Story*.

Mr Saltapple

In *Sea Story*, Purslane and Thrift Saltapple collect salt for their friends in Brambly Hedge. Mr Saltapple likes to relax on the beach in his striped bathing costume.

Mrs Saltapple

Living by the seaside, Thrift Saltapple enjoys the fresh sea breeze in between her salt harvesting chores.

Mr Toadflax

The Toadflax family live in the hornbeam tree and in the *Spring Story*, Mr Toadflax is introduced eating bread and bramble jelly on his doorstep. Later, in the *Winter Story*, he helps organise the Snow Ball.

Mrs Toadflax

Mrs Toadflax is kept very busy in the stories as the mother of Wilfred, Teasel, Clover and Catkin. In the *Winter Story*, she makes some delicious chestnut soup.

Old Mrs Eyebright

Poppy's grandmother, Old Mrs Eyebright, is one of the guests at her wedding in the *Summer Story*. She makes preserves and she can feel bad weather in her bones.

Old Vole

Old Vole lives in a tussock of grass in the middle of the field. In the *Summer Story*, he performs the ceremony at Poppy and Dusty's wedding.

Poppy Eyebright

Poppy Eyebright looks after the Dairy Stump and makes butter and cheese from the milk donated by some friendly cows. In the *Summer Story*, she marries Dusty Dogwood and their family is later featured in *Poppy's Babies*.

Primrose Woodmouse

The daughter of Lord and Lady Woodmouse, Primrose is the bridesmaid in the *Summer Story*. She causes a panic in the *Autumn Story* when she wanders off whilst picking flowers and gets lost. Later, in *The Secret Staircase*, she dresses up with her friend, Wilfred Toadflax, and entertains the Brambly Hedge mice.

Wilfred Toadflax

Wilfred is a mischievous little mouse, full of fun and ideas. In the *Spring Story*, he celebrates his birthday and a picnic is held in his honour. He is the pageboy for the wedding in the *Summer Story*. Later, in *The Secret Staircase*, he and his friend Primrose Woodmouse find some old costumes in the attic of the Old Oak Palace and provide an entertainment for the Brambly Hedge mice.

Teasel

One of the Toadflax children, Teasel chases his sisters, Clover and Catkin, with a snowball in the *Winter Story*. With his brother, Wilfred, he hides under the table at the Snow Ball and eats cream cakes.

ROYAL DOULTON

Mouse group by George Tinworth, c1885.

The Doulton factory was established in the Lambeth area of London in 1815 and, for the first fifty years, John and Henry Doulton concentrated on producing domestic, industrial and sanitary wares. The master of the local school of art in Lambeth encouraged Henry Doulton to experiment with more artistic products and this led to the development of a thriving art pottery studio during the 1870s. By the end of the century, more than three hundred artists were employed decorating vases, figure models and other ornamental pieces. Amongst the novelties of the Victorian period were little groups of mice, which were modelled by the chief artist, George Tinworth. Apparently a family of mice frequently visited his studio and entertained him with their antics. He soon began to visualise them taking part in human pursuits, much to the amusement of Henry Doulton who ordered small editions of his favourite subjects for his friends and customers. Today these whimsical mice groups are amongst the most collectable of all the Lambeth studio wares.

Endowing animals with human attributes was a Victorian preoccupation inspired by Darwin's revelation that the human race descended from apes. Taxidermists responded to the public's fascination by creating elaborate tableaux of stuffed animals wearing the fashions of the day, and popular magazines featured cartoons exploiting the similarities between man and beast. In this climate, it is not surprising to see a succession of anthropomorphic creatures coming from the Lambeth kilns. The interest also spread to Doulton's other factory in Burslem, Stoke-on-Trent, which was acquired in 1877. Initially, tableware and toilet wares were the staple products of this site but the appointment of Charles Noke as chief modeller led to the revival of Staffordshire figures and animal models. During the 1920s and 1930s, he produced a number of animals in human dress, including the Town Mouse and the Country Mouse from *Aesop's Fables* and a set of six Bunnykins figures inspired by the company's best-selling nurseryware.

The Bunnykins figure collection was revived in 1972 shortly after Royal Doulton acquired the John Beswick factory in Longton. This family firm was established in 1894 and, over the years, had achieved a considerable reputation as manufacturers of animal models and novelty items, particularly their longstanding series of figures inspired by

The Town Mouse by Charles Noke, 1920.

Birthday set.

Savings books.

Jill Barklem and Peter Roberts watching a floral being made.

Harry Sales and Jill Barklem.

the tales of Beatrix Potter. During the 1950s and 1960s, Mrs Tittlemouse and Hunca Munca rubbed shoulders with Mickey Mouse and Minnie as the Beswick factory specialised in character merchandise from children's books and films. When Harry Sales was appointed Design Manager of the Beswick studio in 1975, he became responsible for the development of all the character animals and was soon working on another series of mice from the studio of Kitty McBride.

In 1978, Royal Doulton appointed Keith Pybus as their new Marketing Director and he began to cast around for new characters to add to the company's giftware range. When he spotted the article about Brambly Hedge in the *Sunday Times Supplement* of September 1980, he showed it to Harry who was convinced that Jill Barklem's mice would make superb Royal Doulton figures. As Harry later wrote:

'The first time I read the books and studied the illustrations, I felt that I was experiencing something quite unique. Over a period of many years designing for the pottery industry one develops an awareness, a "feeling" for that something special. Brambly Hedge had this.'

Peter Roberts, the Giftware Design Manager, was equally enthusiastic about the possibility of adapting the book illustrations for use on wall plates and other decorative accessories. As soon as permission was received from Jill Barklem's publishers, Harry and Peter set to work on prototype designs.

Understandably, Jill Barklem is very protective of her Brambly Hedge family and prospective licensees are expected to achieve the same high standards that she sets for herself. Fortunately, she was delighted with Harry and Peter's initial designs and relaxed into a productive working relationship as they developed the launch collection. Harry and Peter visited Jill's home to absorb the atmosphere of Brambly Hedge. Together they explored Epping Forest to see the sort of tree stumps that the mice inhabited and they studied Jill's collection of roots, seeds and dried flowers that she uses in her illustrations. Harry later wrote of the visit:

'The weather was dubious and the sky overcast. Jill showed us the inspiration for Crabapple Cottage and we were busily chatting away when it started to rain. We were enveloped in a most unusual light which dramatically emphasised all the shapes and textures of the gnarled old trees and tangled roots. Tiny avenues appeared in the undergrowth, becoming paths for exploration. In the half light one could almost distinguish small doors and the reflected lights became illuminated windows. For a brief moment I felt I was experiencing the real world of Brambly Hedge mice – I half expected to see the little mice scurrying about in raincoats!'

Harry became so absorbed in the world of Brambly Hedge that ideas flowed fast and he soon chose eight launch characters with poses suitable for the ceramic medium. Translating from two dimensions to three is not always so easy because even the most attractive illustrations do not necessarily work well in the round. However, Jill's work is so painstakingly accurate and thorough that it provided all the necessary references for effective translation into clay.

As Harry's staff modellers interpreted his figure designs, Peter Roberts was adapting the cover illustrations from the original Brambly Hedge books to fit a series of collectors plates. With over twenty years experience as a tableware designer, Peter was able to interpret Jill Barklem's style sympathetically for the ceramic printing process. He redrew her illustrations to fit the popular Gainsborough-shaped plate and designed a bramble border

Designs for Brambly Hedge figures by Harry Sales.

evoking each season for the embossed, rococo style rim. He also worked in miniature, reducing floral motifs to feature on the first four thimbles. Jill's delightful title page illustrations suggested the Four Seasons floral ornaments and Peter chose arrangements of buds, blossoms and berries which were assembled petal by petal by Royal Doulton's skilled flower makers.

During the development period, Jill visited the Royal Doulton factories to meet the craftsmen and women who were producing the Brambly Hedge collection and she remembers her delight when she first saw dozens of Primrose figures all looking up at her expectantly as they waited to be decorated. She was fascinated to watch each Brambly Hedge figure being hand-painted in ceramic colours that were carefully researched to match her book illustrations. Then she watched them disappear into the kiln to emerge later with a shiny protective glaze.

The Brambly Hedge collection was launched at the Birmingham International Spring Fair in February 1983 and won a prestigious gift award. The Princess of Wales visited the Royal Doulton stand that year and

Jill prizes a beautiful photograph of the Princess admiring the Brambly Hedge display. She also recalls a wonderful dinner party to mark the launch featuring chestnut soup and other typical Brambly Hedge fare.

Over the next few years, new Brambly Hedge pieces followed in quick succession. Peter adapted Jill's scenes to fit more complicated shapes, such as teapots and bowls, and more illustrations were drawn in the round for collectors plates. Some ideas were more successful than others, for example the Brambly Hedge pendants were not well received by the public and these are amongst the most desirable pieces today. Some designs were made exclusively for overseas markets, such as the teapot warmer and beaker saucers made for Europe. Other ideas never made it into production, for example a Brambly Hedge mobile and mantelpiece clock have been recorded in prototype form.

As Peter's workload increased, he appointed a young graphic designer, Jane James, to assist him with the Brambly Hedge collection and they worked together until Peter's retirement in 1997. Long before Jane joined Royal Doulton she was a fan of the Brambly Hedge stories, so much so that her wedding was inspired by Dusty and Poppy's nuptials in the *Summer Story*. Her wedding cake was based on the three-tiered design in the story and was topped with the

Decorating Brambly Hedge figures.

Winter Story selection.

Design for a mobile by Peter Roberts.

Design for Wilfred Toadflax by Harry Sales.

Design for Mrs Apple by Harry Sales.

Brambly Hedge figures of the bride and groom. Jane's job at Royal Doulton was like a dream come true as she spent much of her time producing graphics for the Brambly Hedge collection. During the 1990s, the range of shapes was expanded considerably to include a variety of teatime and dressing table accessories, all requiring appropriate new artwork from the Brambly Hedge stories. More new designs are currently in development to mark the twentieth anniversary of Brambly Hedge in the year 2000.

Harry Sales continued to expand the figure collection and his next two designs for Mr and Mrs Toadflax were enthusiastically approved by Jill Barklem during a joint radio interview. However, his portrait of Mr Toadflax began to cause problems when it went into production and some of the painters remarked that it was 'rude'! Ironically, the model was a faithful interpretation of the book illustration and nobody had ever suggested that the drawing of the tail was open to misinterpretation. Nevertheless, the mouse's prominent tail was removed shortly after the figure was launched in 1984 and now the original models of Mr Toadflax with tail are very desirable on the secondary market. Collectors also seek out early colour variations of figures such as Poppy Eyebright, Lady Woodmouse and Mrs Toadflax, who carries a bowl of chestnut soup in early examples and carrot soup in later models. The translucent soup was created by combining resin and ceramic, which is technically very difficult to achieve. However, Royal Doulton's technicians worked on a number of resin

Design for Mr Toadflax by Harry Sales.

Ideas for resin figures by Harry Sales.

experiments in the mid-1980s and Harry Sales produced several designs for Brambly Hedge subjects. Sadly, these complex resin models did not materialise and the licence was eventually taken up by Border Fine Arts.

When Harry left Royal Doulton to pursue a freelance career in 1986, the Brambly Hedge figure range became the responsibility of Graham Tongue who added subjects from Jill Barklem's other stories, including *The Secret Staircase*, *The High Hills*, *Sea Story* and *Poppy's Babies*. By 1995, twenty-five figures had been introduced and collectors were surprised when they were all withdrawn two years later. This prompted a lot of activity in the secondary market as collectors rushed to complete their sets and prices have rocketed for early withdrawals and rare variations. The latest news from Royal Doulton is that collectors can look forward to new Brambly Hedge figures in the millennium as designers are working on subjects inspired by the successful animated films.

Design for Old Mrs Eyebright by Harry Sales.

ROYAL DOULTON GIFTWARE

FOUR SEASONS COLLECTION designed by Peter Roberts

Spring Story

'All the mice were up early, but earliest of all was Wilfred Toadflax who lived with his family in the hornbeam tree.'

Summer Story

'Midsummer's Day was picked for the wedding between Poppy Eyebright and Dusty Dogwood and preparations were started at once.'

Autumn Story

'It was very dark inside but Primrose could just see the round front doors set in the walls of the branching passages.'

Winter Story

'The first snowflakes were beginning to fall… "Is that you dear?" called Mrs Apple. Delicious smells wafted down from the kitchen.'
(Text on tea plates and beaker saucers)

Autumn Story selection.

Spring, Summer, Autumn and Winter scenes on each item

Wall plate 1983-C
Thimble 1983-C
Teacup and saucer 1984-C
Tea plate 1984-C
Beaker 1984-C
Beaker saucer 1984-C
Miniature teacup, saucer and plate 1987-1997
Coaster 1989-C
Savings book 1990-C
Trinket box 1990-C
Egg cup 1990-C
Fruit saucer 1990-C
Miniature beaker 1990-1993
Dorothy box 1990-C
Petal bowl 1990-1992
Clover box 1990-1992

Footed bowl 1990-1992
Gainsborough vase, large size 1990-1997
Gainsborough vase, small size, 1991-1993
Powder bowl 1991-1995
Jug and bowl 1991-1997
Cream jug, large size
(This is the same as the jug above and was sold separately in some markets)

Oatmeal bowl 1991-C
(This is the same as the basin above and was sold separately in some markets)
Picture frame 1992-1995
Hinged box 1992-1995

SPRING COLLECTION

Top row: savings book, petal bowl, picture frame. Bottom row: tea plate, Gainsborough vase, small size, fruit saucer.

Top row: trinket box (hinged) coaster behind, trinket box, Clover box. Bottom row: miniature teacup and saucer, Dorothy box, miniature beaker and tea plate.

Top row: Gainsborough vase, large size, eggcup, footed bowl. Middle row: powder bowl, jug and bowl. Bottom row: teacup and saucer, beaker.

SUMMER COLLECTION

Top row: Gainsborough vase, small size, powder bowl, fruit saucer. Bottom row: footed bowl, Gainsborough vase, large size, jug and bowl.

Top row: trinket box, petal bowl, eggcup, coaster. Bottom row: miniature teacup, saucer, tea plate and beaker, teacup and saucer, trinket box (hinged).

Top row: Clover box, Dorothy box. Middle row: picture frame, beaker. Bottom row: tea plate, savings book.

AUTUMN COLLECTION

Top row: Clover box, trinket box (hinged), miniature beaker, tea plate, teacup and saucer.
Bottom row: trinket box, fruit saucer, coaster.

Top row: teacup and saucer, petal bowl, beaker. Bottom row: tea plate, Gainsborough vase, large size, picture frame.

AUTUMN COLLECTION

Top row: powder bowl, eggcup, Dorothy box. Middle row: Gainsborough vase, small size, savings book. Bottom row: jug and bowl, footed bowl.

WINTER COLLECTION

Top row: teacup and saucer, powder bowl, savings book. Bottom row: Gainsborough vase, small size, tea plate, fruit saucer.

Top row; miniature teacup and saucer, tea plate and beaker, Clover box, eggcup, trinket box (hinged). Bottom row: footed bowl, petal bowl, trinket box.

WINTER COLLECTION

Top row: Dorothy box, coaster. Middle row: beaker, picture frame. Bottom row: Gainsborough vase, large size, jug and bowl.

THE PICNIC (*Spring Story*) designed by Peter Roberts

'When tea was over, the grown ups snoozed under the bluebells whilst the young mice played hide and seek in the primroses.' (Text on wall plate)

'Here we are cried Lord Woodmouse at last. The baskets were put down and opened, and nettlestem cloths spread out on the mossy grass. In no time at all, the food was unpacked.' (Text on sandwich tray)

Sandwich tray 1989-1993
Wall plate 1990-1993
Gainsborough vase, large size, 1989-1993

THE BIRTHDAY (*Spring Story*) designed by Peter Roberts

'"Happy Birthday, Wilfred," said Mrs and Mrs Toadflax sleepily. He tore off the pretty wrappings, and scattered them all over the floor.'
(Text on wall plate)

Trinket box 1987-1995
Miniature teacup, saucer and plate 1990-1992

Children's teacup, saucer and tea plate 1990-1993
Miniature trinket box 1990-1992
Teacup and saucer 1987-C
Beaker 1989-C
Miniature beaker 1990-1992
Wall plate 1987-C

BREAKFAST AND TEATIME (*Spring Story*) designed by Peter Roberts

'They found Mr Apple in the kitchen drinking mint tea with Mrs Crustybread.' (Text on bread and butter plate, Regal tray and teapot)

Miniature teapot, sugar and cream 1987-1998
Sugar bowl 1987-C

Regal tray 1990-C
Cream jug 1987-C
Marmalade pot 1990-1997
Coffee pot 1990-1997
Teapot 1987-C

Lamp 1990-1991
Clock with Harvest Mice (*Autumn Story*) 1989-C

Teapot warmer 1995-C (European market only)

Sandwich tray 1990-C (European market only)

Teapot warmer in use.

Bread and butter plate 1990-C

THE WEDDING (*Summer Story*) designed by Peter Roberts

'Poppy Eyebright do you love Dusty Dogwood and will you love him and care for him for ever and ever? Poppy vowed that she would.' (Text on wall plate)

Miniature trinket box 1990-1992
Miniature teacup, saucer and plate 1990-1992
Miniature beaker 1990-1992

Wall plate 1987-C
Beaker 1989-C
Teacup and saucer 1987-C
Trinket box 1987-1995

THE ENGAGEMENT *(Summer Story)* designed by Peter Roberts

'Early in June, Miss Poppy Eyebright and Mr Dusty Dogwood officially announced their engagement. Everyone along the hedgerow was delighted.' (Text on wall plate)

Teacup and saucer 1989-1997
Wall plate 1989-1997
Trinket box 1989-1995
Beaker 1992-1997

POPPY'S BABIES *(Poppy's Babies)* designed by Jane James

'The buds on the branches blossom and flower,
The blackbirds sing in the leafy bower,
And over the hills comes the rising sun,
To shine on the fields and you little one.'
(Text on wall plate)

Teacup and saucer 1997-C
Wall plate 1997-C
Trinket box 1997-C
Beaker 1997-C

POPPY'S BEDROOM (*Summer Story*) designed by Peter Roberts

'In her room above the dairy, Poppy dressed carefully. She peeped at her reflection in the shiny wardrobe door, took a deep breath, and ran downstairs to join her bridesmaids.' (Text on Regal tray)

Powder bowl 1991-1994
Picture frame 1991-1994

Posy vase 1991-1994
Regal tray 1991-1994
Ring stand 1991-1993
Dorothy box 1991-1994
Pin tray 1991-1993

MERRY MIDWINTER *(Winter Story)* **designed by Peter Roberts**

'The eating and drinking and dancing carried on late into the night. At midnight, all the hedgerow children were taken home to bed.' (Text on plates)

Candlestick 1995-1997
Wall plate 1995-1997
Beaker 1995-1997

Tea plate 1995-1997
Teacup and saucer 1995-1997,

ANNUALS

Spring Story 1996

'Lord Woodmouse, meanwhile, was working his way down to the stream. The news had travelled ahead of him, and all along the hedge excited mice leaned out of their windows to ask when the picnic would take place.' (Text on wall plate)

Wall plate
Teacup and saucer

Autumn Story 1998

'It was a fine autumn. The blackberries were ripe, and the nuts were ready, and the mice of Brambly Hedge were very busy. Primrose picked the berries nearest the ground while her father hooked the upper branches down with his walking stick.'

Wall plate
Teacup and saucer

Summer Story 1997

'Out of doors, the best place to be was down by the stream. The mice gathered there in the afternoon, sat under the bank in the shade, and dangled their paws and tails in the clear water.' (Text on wall plate)

Teacup and saucer
Wall plate

Winter Story 1999

'The eating and drinking and dancing carried on late into the night. At midnight, all the hedgerow children were taken home to bed. As soon as they were safely tucked up, their parents returned to the Ball.'

Wall plate
Teacup and saucer

SURPRISE OUTING COLLECTION *(Spring Story)*

1995-C (still current) This collection was exclusive to Europe and Canada.

The Invitation teacup and saucer
The Plan teacup and saucer

The Outing teacup and saucer
The Meeting teacup and saucer

INTERIORS COLLECTION

1994-C This collection was exclusive to Europe.

The Store Stump teacup and saucer (*Spring Story*)
The Dairy teacup and saucer (*Summer Story*)
Old Oak Palace teacup and saucer (*Autumn Story*)
Crabapple Cottage teacup and saucer (*Winter Story*)

FLORALS

Spring Posy 1983-1989
Summer Bouquet 1983-1989
Autumn Basket 1983-1989
Winter Hollow 1983-1989

JEWELLERY

Silver pendants 1984-1986
Wilfred Toadflax *(Spring Story)*
Dusty Dogwood *(Summer Story)* (not illustrated)
Poppy Eyebright *(Summer Story)* (not illustrated)
Primrose Woodmouse *(Autumn Story)*

Gold Pendants 22ct 1984-1986
Spring
Summer

THIMBLES

Wilfred (*Spring Story*) 1984-1992
'*Wilfred stood up and played Hickory Dickory Dandelion Clock on his new whistle.*'

Mrs Apple (*Spring Story*) 1984-1992
'*At last the sun began to sink behind the far woods, it was time to go home.*'

The Wedding (*Summer Story*) 1984-1992
'*All the mice cheered as Dusty kissed his wife and the bridesmaid threw baskets of petals over the happy couple.*'

Basil (*Summer Story*) 1984-1992
'*Basil selected some white wines, primrose, meadowsweet and elderflower, and hung them to cool in the rushes.*'

Primrose Sleeping (*Autumn Story*) 1984-1992
'*Her mother gave Primrose a kiss and smoothed her pillow.*'

Lady Woodmouse (*Autumn Story*) 1984-1992
'*"Oh Dear!" said Lady Daisy. Primrose is such a little mouse. Where can she be?*'

Clover (*Winter Story*) 1984-1992
'*Mrs Toadflax put fresh wood on the fire and set Clover to work with the toasting fork.*'

The Little Children (*Winter Story*) 1984-1992
'*The children climbed out of their bunk beds to watch the snowflakes falling past the window.*'

Spring 1983-C
Summer 1983-C
Autumn 1983-C
Winter 1983-C

WALL PLATES
FOUR SEASONS COLLECTION designed by Peter Roberts

1983-C

Spring

'It was the most beautiful morning. The spring sunshine crept into every cottage along Brambly Hedge, and the little windows in the trees were open wide…It was Wilfred's birthday.'

Autumn

'Hidden in the brambles, Primrose discovered a very interesting hole. "I wonder if anyone lives down there," she said to herself, and wandered into the tunnel.'

Summer

'Early that summer, Miss Poppy Eyebright and Mr Dusty Dogwood officially announced their engagement. Everyone along the hedgerow was delighted.'

Winter

'Mrs Apple had spent the afternoon baking pies, cakes and pudding for the cold days to come. She drew two armchairs up to the fire, and brought in Mr Apple's supper on a tray.'

WALL PLATES
MIDWINTER'S EVE COLLECTION designed by Peter Roberts

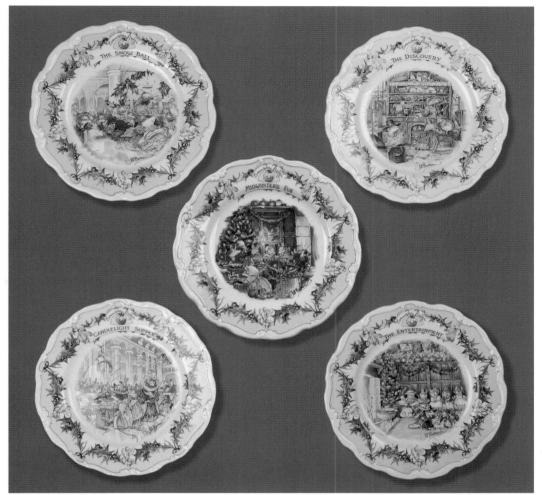

The Snow Ball (*Winter Story*) 1984-1991
'*Basil struck up a jolly tune on his violin and the dancing began. All the dances were very fast and twirly and were made even faster by the slippery ice floor.*'

Candlelight Supper (*Winter Story*) 1986-1991
'*Wilfred and Teasel crept under a table to watch and every now and then, a little paw appeared and a cream cake disappeared.*

The Discovery (*The Secret Staircase*) 1985-1991
'*Wilfred peered inside an ancient trunk and pulled out dresses and cloaks, waistcoats and shawls, some trimmed with gold and others studded with shining stones.*'

The Entertainment (*The Secret Staircase*) 1987-1991
'*Primrose and Wilfred threw off their cloaks and donned their hats with a flourish. The audience gasped to see the beautiful clothes which sparkled in the firelight and then clapped and cheered louder than ever.*'

Midwinter's Eve (*The Secret Staircase*) 1983-1992 for Lawleys by Post
'*That evening after dark, all the mice would gather round a blazing fire for the traditional Midwinter celebrations. A grand entertainment was planned and Primrose and Wilfred had chosen to give a recitation.*'

WALL PLATES

THE INTERIORS COLLECTION designed by Peter Roberts

1986-1997

The Store Stump (*Spring Story*)
'*Wilfred's legs felt tired and he sat down by the fire to rest. Mr Apple lifted down a jar of sugared violets and filled a twist of paper with sweets.*'

Old Oak Palace (*Autumn Story*)
'*Primrose was nearly asleep by the time they got home. A clean nightie was warming by the fire and a mug of hot acorn coffee had been placed by the bed.*'

The Dairy (*Summer Story*)
'*The wedding day dawned at last. In her room above the dairy, Poppy dressed carefully. She polished her whiskers and dabbed rosewater behind her ears.*'

Crabapple Cottage (*Winter Story*)
'*Clover and Catkin helped Mrs Apple string crabapples to roast over the fire. The boys had to sit and watch because they ate too many.*'

WALL PLATES

THE SECRET STAIRCASE COLLECTION designed by Peter Roberts

1990-1996 All from *The Secret Staircase*

The Palace Kitchen

'Lady Woodmouse was busy making caraway biscuits in the kitchen. She leaned on her rolling pin to listen to Primrose's tale of woe. "Why don't you see if there's something up in the attics for you to wear," she said.'

The Great Hall

'"Why don't you take off your cloak, dear?" said Lady Woodmouse. "It's very hot here by the fire." "Not just yet," Mama," said Primrose. "I'm still a bit chilly."'

The Grand Bathroom

'There was a dining room, a butler's pantry, a small kitchen and several other bedrooms. The bathroom was particularly grand with a tiled floor and high windows.'

The Forgotten Room

'Primrose and Wilfred went from room to room looking for a suitable spot for their rehearsal. They ended up in a crowded storeroom at the end of a passage, but it was difficult to concentrate on practising, there were so many things to look at.'

WALL PLATES

PRIMROSE'S ADVENTURE COLLECTION designed by Peter Roberts

1991-1995 All from the *Autumn Story*

Where's Primrose

'Lord and Lady Woodmouse decided to help pick mushrooms, and they were just setting off when Lady Woodmouse cried out in alarm, "Where's Primrose?" She was nowhere to be seen.'

The Adventure

'Meanwhile, Primrose, wandering along the edge of the cornfield, was quite unaware of her parents' concern. She was just going to help a group of mice gathering seeds in the ditch, when she spotted a little round house high in the stalks of corn. "I wonder who lives there."'

The Search Party

'The children thought she was at her grandmother's house and a search party was sent along to investigate. "Have you seen Primrose?" asked Wilfred. "We've lost her." Mrs Apple shook her head, took off her apron and joined in the search.

Safe at Last

'"Mr Apple!" she squeaked with delight. As each of the figures turned round she recognised them: Mr Apple, Mrs Apple, Dusty Dogwood, and best of all, her own mother and father. Primrose pushed her way through the brambles. "Primrose!" cried Lady Daisy. "You're safe."

WALL PLATES

SURPRISE OUTING COLLECTION designed by Peter Roberts

1993-1997 All from the *Spring Story*

The Plan

'"We thought it would be nice to have a surprise picnic for your Wilfred," whispered Mr Apple. "We won't tell them what it's for, and we'll all meet at midday by the Palace roots." Mr Toadflax was delighted with the suggestion and went inside to tell his wife.'

The Meeting

'When the Toadflax family arrived at the Palace, Wilfred was rather disappointed that no one there seemed to know it was his birthday. Indeed he had hoped for a few more presents but it would have been rude to drop hints, so he hid his feelings as best he could.'

The Invitation

'Lord Woodmouse, meanwhile, was working his way down to the stream. The news had travelled ahead of him, and all along the hedge excited mice leaned out of their windows to ask when the picnic would take place. "Shall we bring tablecloths?" called the weavers who lived in the tangly hawthorn trees.'

The Outing

'At a signal from Lord Woodmouse, they all set off with their baskets, hampers and wheelbarrows. It was a very long way. Heaving and pulling, wheeling and hauling, the mice made their way round the Palace, through the cornfield and up by the stream.'

SHAPE GUIDE

Wall plate, D 8ins (20.5cms) 1983-C
Thimble 1983-C, H 1^1/$_4$ins (3cms)
Beaker 1984-C, H 3^1/$_2$ins (9cms)
Beaker Saucer 1984-C, D 6^1/$_2$ins (16.5cms)
  (European market only)
Teacup and saucer 1984-C, H 3ins (7.5cms)
Children's teacup and saucer 1990-1993, H 2^1/$_2$ins
  (6.5cms)
Tea plate 1984-C, D 6ins (15.5cms)
Teapot 1987-C, H 6^1/$_2$ins (16.5cms)
Sugar bowl 1987-C, H 2ins (5cms)
Cream jug 1987-C, H 3^1/$_2$ins (9cms)
Coaster 1989-C, D 4^3/$_4$ins (12cms)
Gainsborough vase, large size, 1990-1997, H 6^1/$_2$ins
  (16.5cms)
Gainsborough vase, small size, 1991-1993, H 5ins
  (12.5cms)
Sandwich tray 1989-C, W 11^3/$_4$ins (30cms)
Trinket box 1990-C, H 1^1/$_4$ins (3.5cms)
Clock 1989-C, H 8ins (20.5cms)
Savings book 1990-C, H 5ins (12.5cms)
Egg cup 1990-C, H 2^1/$_4$ins (5.5cms)
Bread and butter plate 1990-C, W 10^1/$_2$ins (26.5cms)
Coffee pot 1990-1997, H 8^1/$_2$ins (21.5cms)
Fruit saucer 1990-C, D 5^1/$_2$ins (14cms)
Marmalade pot 1990-1997, H 4^1/$_2$ins (10.5cms)
Regal tray 1990-C, W 10ins (25.5cms)
Lamp 1990-1991, H 8ins (20.5cms)
Dorothy box 1990-C, H 3ins (7.5cms)
Clover box 1990-1992, H 2ins (5cms)
Petal bowl 1990-1992, H 2^1/$_4$ins (5.5cms)
Footed bowl 1990-1992, H 3^1/$_4$ins (8cms)
Teapot warmer 1995-C , H 2^1/$_2$ins (6.5cms)
  (European market only)
Picture frame 1991-1995, H 5ins (12.5cms)
Powder bowl 1991-1995, H 4^1/$_4$ins (10.5cms)
Pin tray 1991-1993, D 3^1/$_2$ins (9cms)
Posy vase 1991-C, H 3^1/$_4$ins (8cms) as
  Gainsborough vase, small size
Ring stand 1991-1993, H 2^1/$_4$ins (5.5cms)
Jug and bowl 1991-1997, H 4^1/$_4$ins (11cms)
Cream jug, large size, 1991-C, H 4^1/$_4$ins (11cms),
  (as jug above)
Hinged box 1992-1995, H 1^1/$_2$ins (4cms)
Candlestick 1995-1997, H 2^1/$_4$ins (5.5cms)
Oatmeal bowl 1991-C, H 4^1/$_4$ins (11cms),
  (as bowl above)

MINIATURES

Miniature teapot, cream jug and sugar bowl 1987-1997, H 4ins (10cms)
Miniature teacup, saucer and plate 1987-1997
  H 1^1/$_2$ins (4cms)
Miniature beaker 1990-1993, H 1^3/$_4$ins (4.5cms)
Miniature trinket box 1990-1992, D 2ins (5cms)

FLORALS

Spring Posy 1983-1989, H 2^1/$_4$ins (5.5cms)
Summer Bouquet 1983-1989, H 2^1/$_4$ins (5.5cms)
Autumn Basket 1983-1989, H 2^1/$_4$ins (5.5cms)
Winter Hollow 1983-1989, H 2^3/$_4$ins (7cms)

JEWELLERY

Silver pendant 1984-1986, D 1in (2.5cms)
Gold pendant 1984-1986, D 1in (2.5cms)

Autumn Collection showing comparative size of the oatmeal bowl and fruit saucer.

Beaker and saucer with teacup and saucer.

Plate 8ins

Plate 6ins

Teacup and Saucer

Beaker

Eggcup

Fruit Saucer

Miniature Beaker

Miniature Afternoon Tea Set

Coaster

Thimble

Savings Book

Picture Frame

Trinket Box

Trinket Box (hinged)

Dorothy Box

Petal Bowl

Clover Box

Footed Bowl

Gainsborough Vase, large size

Powder Bowl

Gainsborough Vase, small size (also known as Posy Vase)

Bowl and Jug, small size

Coffee Pot

Teapot

Teapot Warmer

Cream and Sugar Bowl

Bread and Butter Plate

Sandwich Tray

Oatmeal Saucer

Miniature Teapot, Cream and Sugar Bowl

Marmalade Pot

Candlestick

Clock

Lamp Base

Regal Tray

Ring Stand

Pin Tray

ROYAL DOULTON FIGURES

DBH1 Poppy Eyebright

Story	*Summer Story*
Designer	Harry Sales
Modeller	David Lyttleton
Height	3¼ins (8cms)
Introduced	1983
Withdrawn	1997

In early examples of this figure, Poppy wears a pink wedding dress.

DBH2 Mr Apple

Story	*Winter Story*
Designer	Harry Sales
Modeller	David Lyttleton
Height	3¼ins (8cms)
Introduced	1983
Withdrawn	1997

DBH3 Mrs Apple

Story	*Winter Story*
Designer	Harry Sales
Modeller	David Lyttleton
Height	3¼ins (8cms)
Introduced	1983
Withdrawn	1997

DBH4 Lord Woodmouse

Story	*Autumn Story*
Designer	Harry Sales
Modeller	David Lyttleton
Height	3¼ins (8cms)
Introduced	1983
Withdrawn	1997

DBH5 Lady Woodmouse

Story	*Autumn Story*
Designer	Harry Sales
Modeller	David Lyttleton
Height	3¼ins (8cms)
Introduced	1983
Withdrawn	1997

DBH6 Dusty Dogwood

Story	*Summer Story*
Designer	Harry Sales
Modeller	David Lyttleton
Height	3¼ins (8cms)
Introduced	1983
Withdrawn	1997

DBH7 Wilfred Toadflax

Story	*Spring Story*
Designer	Harry Sales
Modeller	David Lyttleton
Height	3¼ins (8cms)
Introduced	1983
Withdrawn	1997

DBH8 Primrose Woodmouse

Story	*Autumn Story*
Designer	Harry Sales
Modeller	David Lyttleton
Height	3¼ins (8cms)
Introduced	1983
Withdrawn	1997

DBH9 Old Mrs Eyebright

Story	*Summer Story*
Designer	Harry Sales
Modeller	David Lyttleton
Height	3¼ins (8cms)
Introduced	1984
Withdrawn	1995

Different versions of Lady Woodmouse.

Top row: DBH1, DBH2, DBH3. Middle row: DBH4, DBH5, DBH6. Bottom row: DBH7, DBH8, DBH9.

DBH10 Mr Toadflax

Story	*Spring Story*
Designer	Harry Sales
Modeller	David Lyttleton
Height	3¹/₄ins (8cms)
Introduced	1984
Withdrawn	1997

There are three versions of this figure. In the first, the tail is at the front. In the second, the tail is at the back and there is no cushion. In the third, the cushion has been replaced and the tail is at the side.

DBH11 Mrs Toadflax

Story	*Winter Story*
Designer	Harry Sales
Modeller	David Lyttleton
Height	3¹/₄ins (8cms)
Introduced	1985
Withdrawn	1995

DBH12 Catkin

Story	*Winter Story*
Designer	Harry Sales
Modeller	David Lyttleton
Height	3¹/₄ins (8cms)

Introduced 1985
Withdrawn 1994

DBH13 Old Vole

Story	*Summer Story*
Designer	Harry Sales
Modeller	David Lyttleton
Height	3¹/₄ins (8cms)
Introduced	1985
Withdrawn	1992

DBH14 Basil

Story	*Summer Story*
Designer	Harry Sales
Modeller	David Lyttleton
Height	3¹/₄ins (8cms)
Introduced	1985
Withdrawn	1992

DBH15 Mrs Crustybread

Story	*Spring Story*
Designer	Graham Tongue
Modeller	Ted Chawner
Height	3¹/₄ins (8cms)
Introduced	1987
Withdrawn	1994

DBH16 Clover

Story	*Winter Story*
Designer	Graham Tongue
Modeller	Graham Tongue
Height	3¹/₄ins (8cms)
Introduced	1987
Withdrawn	1997

DBH17 Teasel

Story	*Winter Story*
Designer	Graham Tongue
Modeller	Ted Chawner
Height	3¹/₄ins (8cms)
Introduced	1987
Withdrawn	1992

DBH18 The Store Stump Money Box

Story	*Spring Story*
Designer	Harry Sales
Modeller	Martyn Alcock
Height	3¹/₄ins (8cms)
Introduced	1987
Withdrawn	1989

Mr Toadflax, version 1, 1984.

Mr Toadflax, version 2, 1984-85.

Mr Toadflax, version 3, 1985-97.

Top row: DBH10, DBH11, DBH12. Middle row: DBH13, DBH14, DBH15. Bottom row: DBH16, DBH18, DBH17.

DBH19 Lily Weaver

Story	*The High Hills*
Designer	Graham Tongue
Modeller	Ted Chawner
Height	3$\frac{1}{4}$ins (8cms)
Introduced	1988
Withdrawn	1993

DBH20 Flax Weaver

Story	*The High Hills*
Designer	Graham Tongue
Modeller	Ted Chawner
Height	3$\frac{1}{4}$ins (8cms)
Introduced	1988
Withdrawn	1993

DBH21 Conker

Story	*Summer Story*
Designer	Graham Tongue
Modeller	Ted Chawner
Height	3$\frac{1}{4}$ins (8cms)
Introduced	1988
Withdrawn	1994

DBH22 Primrose Entertains

Story	*The Secret Staircase*
Designer	Graham Tongue
Modeller	Alan Maslankowski
Height	3$\frac{1}{4}$ins (8cms)
Introduced	1990
Withdrawn	1995

DBH23 Wilfred Entertains

Story	*The Secret Staircase*
Designer	Graham Tongue
Modeller	Alan Maslankowski
Height	3$\frac{1}{4}$ins (8cms)
Introduced	1990
Withdrawn	1995

DBH24 Mr Saltapple

Story	*Sea Story*
Designer	Graham Tongue
Modeller	Warren Platt
Height	2$\frac{1}{4}$ins (5.5cms)
Introduced	1993
Withdrawn	1997

DBH25 Mrs Saltapple

Story	*Sea Story*
Designer	Graham Tongue
Modeller	Warren Platt
Height	3$\frac{1}{2}$ins (9cms)
Introduced	1993
Withdrawn	1997

DBH26 Dusty and Baby

Story	*Poppy's Babies*
Designer	Graham Tongue
Modeller	Martyn Alcock
Height	2$\frac{3}{4}$ins (7cms)
Introduced	1995
Withdrawn	1997

Top row: DBH19, DBH20, DBH21. Middle row: DBH22, DBH23. Bottom row: DBH26, DBH24, DBH25.

ROYAL DOULTON

MELAMINE

Designed by Jane James

Mrs Apple's kitchen accessories were introduced in 1994 and withdrawn in 1997.

Chopping board
Rectangular tray
Round tray

TEXTILES

These kitchen accessories were introduced in 1994 and withdrawn in 1997.

Oven mitt
Double oven mitt
Napkins (6)
Place mats (2)
Apron
Tea towel
Tea cosy
Round tablecloth
Rectangular tablecloth

PRINTS

These Four Seasons framed prints were signed by Jill Barklem and featured in the Lawleys by Post catalogue in 1994.

Spring Story
Summer Story
Autumn Story
Winter Story

BORDER FINE ARTS AND ENESCO

Border Fine Arts was founded by John Hammond in 1974 following a brief visit to the Scottish Borders. Whilst on holiday in the Lake District, he drove up to Scotland for the day just to say he'd been there. On his return, the weather deteriorated and dense fog enveloped his car. Visibility became so poor that he decided to stop for the night and he found a little guesthouse in Langholm, twenty-two miles north of Carlisle. The next morning he explored the tranquil little town on the banks of the River Esk and was so impressed by the warmth and friendliness of the community that he began to investigate the possibility of living there. He asked to be kept informed of any property that appeared on the market and eventually Middleholms Farm came up for sale.

John Hammond moved north and started a new business producing hand-crafted studies of local wildlife and farm animals. From humble beginnings around the kitchen table, Border Fine Arts gradually grew into a highly successful company, renowned for the quality of its animal subjects. Helping to build this reputation was Ray Ayres, the head of the design department, who joined the company in 1976 after graduating from the Southampton and Winchester schools of art. Initially, bronze was the medium for his animal studies, but it soon became apparent that collectors preferred more colourful designs so the company began to introduce hand-painted figurines in the late 1970s. One of Ray's most successful collections in the early years featured an impudent house mouse sampling different types of fruit, so the painters gained a lot of experience portraying these tiny creatures.

The Border Fine Arts sculptures are cast in a resin type material that retains the most intricate details of feathers and fur so it is ideal for showing off the skills of the artists to best

advantage. Each subject is extensively researched to ensure anatomical accuracy and the artists travel all over the country seeking information from animal breeders, ornithologists, farmers and pet owners. Over the years they have worked closely with conservation societies including the Worldwide Fund for Nature, and the Wildfowl and Wetlands Trust, to ensure a better future for the species they depict. Agricultural subjects have always been very successful for the company, particularly the groups inspired by James Herriot's famous books about his career as a Yorkshire vet for which the company holds an exclusive licence.

In 1987, John Hammond began to think about reproducing the work of other well-known animal writers and he had examples of Beatrix Potter's illustrations on his desk during a meeting with Richard Wawrzesta, the Managing Director of Chiltern, a BFA subsidiary company in Northampton. Richard's expertise was production, so John was surprised when he asked if he could try modelling some Beatrix Potter subjects. Although Richard had studied at art school and dabbled in several artistic ventures before joining Chiltern, he had done very little modelling. Nevertheless, he felt intuitively that he could give Peter Rabbit and Hunca Munca a

Jill Barklem, Richard Wawrzesta and Karen Addison.

Richard Wawrzesta at the Tabletalk event.

new lease of life and set to work modelling in wax, his preferred medium. Frederick Warne, the publishers, were very pleased with his prototypes and Copyrights licensed Border Fine Arts to produce a collection of Beatrix Potter figures. Although portraying animals in human dress was a new direction for the company, collectors responded with enthusiasm and the collection is still going strong today.

Encouraged by his success with the tales of Beatrix Potter, Richard next tried his hand at some of the residents of Brambly Hedge. He was introduced to Jill Barklem's stories by Karen Addison, who had recently joined Border Fine Arts from Royal Doulton where she had seen the success of the Brambly Hedge characters in ceramic. Together they had a meeting with Jill Barklem to seek approval for Richard's first models and they received an enthusiastic reception. Jill was particularly impressed with all the diminutive detail that could be achieved in the resin medium used by Border Fine Arts. Tiny fruits and flowers, teacups and toys could all be incorporated in the little figures and the texture of the skin and fur was incredibly realistic. As well as the mouse figures, Richard also modelled furniture from the Brambly Hedge illustrations and here too he could revel in Jill's great love of detail. His Store Stump

kitchen table groans under the weight of mouse-size delicacies and the shelves of the dresser are stacked with pots of jam, recipe books and pieces of the best blue and white china. As with the books, collectors can study his work for hours, making new discoveries at every turn. Look closely to see the grains of corn that have been dropped on the kitchen floor or the minute candied fruits on top of Poppy and Dusty's wedding cake. Jill has always been very interested in food and so she was particularly thrilled that all the pies, cakes and jellies in Richard's designs looked good enough to eat even though they measure less than half-a-centimetre in diameter.

Jill was so delighted with Richard's designs that a licence was granted to Border Fine Arts in January 1987 and a year later the Store Stump Kitchen Collection was launched. Richard and Jill were invited to make a joint appearance at a special retail promotion for Tabletalk in Brentwood and, whilst Jill autographed copies of her books and chatted to collectors, Richard amazed the audience with his ability to model rapidly and talk about his work at the same time. He is very modest about his extraordinary talents but then he has four children to help keep his feet firmly on the ground. They were his chief critics when they were young and his son, Alex, was always particularly interested in Wilfred's exploits. Perhaps this is why Wilfred features in so many different guises in the Border Fine Arts collection: acting as a pageboy in the wedding party, reciting at the Midwinter celebrations, jigging in the nursery and playing with his toys at his birthday picnic.

The early Border Fine Arts figures were packaged in eye-catching tin boxes which are desirable in their own right. Originally, customers could also purchase cardboard display stands that provided appropriate settings for the figures and furniture but they were withdrawn by 1992 and are difficult to find today. In 1990, some of the best-loved characters were mounted on musical bases which proved to be popular gifts and later Richard extended the Brambly Hedge range to include clocks, cameos, water balls and picture frames. These novelty gifts were developed in collaboration with the Enesco Corporation of Illinois, USA, which became associated with Border Fine Arts in 1989.

Enesco was founded in 1958 as a division of N. Shure Company and takes its name from the initials of its original company N.S.Co. In the last forty years, it has become one of the world's leading producers of fine gifts, collectables and decorative accessories and Border Fine Arts became distributors of Enesco products in the UK. There are over 12,000 items in the Enesco range, including famous collections such as *Precious Moments, Cherished Teddies* and *Musical Masterpieces*. In 1989, Enesco added to their portfolio by securing a licence to produce Brambly Hedge designs, primarily for the US market, and Richard Wawrzesta's models were used as prototypes for their resin figures. These were produced in China for distribution in the USA and at first glance they are identical to the Border Fine Arts models, except that the Chinese resin body has a waxier finish. As with Border Fine Arts, the Enesco resin figures were also incorporated into water balls and musicals but the range was more extensive and included musicals of Wilfred and Primrose on treasure chests and an elaborate wedding tableau.

A huge party was organised by Enesco to launch the Brambly Hedge collection and their Illinois showroom was transformed for the occasion. Jill Barklem travelled to the USA as the guest of honour and retailers flew in from all over the country to meet her and see the new range. Following the launch of the Enesco resin figures, Richard Wawrzesta was also commissioned to model miniature pewter figures and thimbles and these were manufactured in China and Taiwan. To display the tiny pewter pieces, he designed a resin store stump 'house' derived from Jill's detailed cross-sections of mouse buildings and this is very sought after today. As the pewter figures did not conflict with the existing Border Fine Arts figures, they were distributed in the UK together with other Brambly Hedge products commissioned overseas by Enesco, such as

decorative tins and Jack-in-the-Boxes incorporating plush toys. New designs were added to Enesco's Brambly Hedge range until 1992 and the entire collection had been withdrawn by 1994. However, Richard continued to develop the Brambly Hedge collection for Border Fine Arts after that date and the publication of *Poppy's Babies* in 1994 provided him with the inspiration for an entirely new collection of figures.

The Midwinter display.

In November 1995, the successful partnership between the American and Scottish companies was cemented when Enesco bought Border Fine Arts. The packaging for the last Brambly Hedge accessories, such as the tree stump bookends and the cradle money box, indicates that Border Fine Arts is a registered UK trademark of the Enesco European Giftware Group. A year later the entire Brambly Hedge collection was discontinued by Border Fine Arts and fans are now scurrying around trying to complete their sets. In the UK, the most elusive Border Fine Arts figures appear to be Lord and Lady Woodmouse Resting, Mrs Apple and Wilfred. A very rare colour variation of Clover and Teasel has also been recorded where Teasel wears a red-striped jumper instead of the standard blue. Many of the Enesco products are hard to find in the UK and there seems to be some confusion in the marketplace because of the similarity to the Border designs. Sadly, there are few records at Enesco to clarify matters and the listings in this book have been pieced together from surviving brochures or catalogues.

BORDER FINE ARTS

The licence was issued in January 1987 and expired December 1997. The entire collection was modelled by Richard Wawrzesta and the first eight figures were launched in 1988. The figures are impressed at the back 'B.H. c J.B. date year (e.g. 1989) B.F.A. There is also a paper label on the bottom of the base. The first figures were packaged in metal tins and the furniture in cardboard boxes. Later figures were packaged in cardboard boxes. Border Fine Arts was acquired by Enesco in November 1995 and there is sometimes a reference to Enesco on the packaging after this date.

THE STORE STUMP KITCHEN COLLECTION

BH1 Mrs Apple
Series	The Store Stump Kitchen
Story	*Spring Story*
Height	2¹/₂ins (6.5cms)
Introduced	1988
Withdrawn	1996

BH2 Lady Woodmouse
Series	The Store Stump Kitchen
Story	*Spring Story*
Height	2¹/₂ins (6.5cms)
Introduced	1988
Withdrawn	1995

BH3 Primrose
Series	The Store Stump Kitchen
Story	*Spring Story*
Height	2¹/₄ins (5.5cms)
Introduced	1988
Withdrawn	1996

BH4 Wilfred
Series	The Store Stump Kitchen
Story	*Spring Story*
Height	2¹/₂ins (6.5cms)
Introduced	1988
Withdrawn	1996

BH5 Mr Apple in Rocking Chair
Series	The Store Stump Kitchen
Story	*Spring Story*
Height	3¹/₄ins (8cms)
Introduced	1988
Withdrawn	1995

BH6 The Dresser
Series	The Store Stump Kitchen
Story	*Spring Story*
Height	5ins (12.5cms)
Introduced	1988
Withdrawn	1995

BH7 The Table
Series	The Store Stump Kitchen
Story	*Spring Story*

Height	3ins (7.5cms)
Introduced	1988
Withdrawn	1995

BH8 The Fireplace
Series	The Store Stump Kitchen
Story	*Spring Story*
Height	5ins (12.5cms)
Introduced	1988
Withdrawn	1995

BH25 Mrs Crustybread with Mixing Bowl
Series	The Store Stump Kitchen
Story	*Spring Story*
Height	2¹/₂ins (6.5cms)
Introduced	1991
Withdrawn	1996

BH26 Basil with Bottles
Series	The Store Stump Kitchen
Story	*Summer Story*
Height	2¹/₂ins (6.5cms)
Introduced	1991
Withdrawn	1996

THE STORE STUMP KITCHEN COLLECTION

Top row: BH2, BH3, BH4, BH5, BH1. Middle row: BH25, BH7, BH26. Bottom row: BH8, BH6.

THE WEDDING COLLECTION

BH9 Poppy Eyebright - Bride
Series	The Wedding
Story	*Summer Story*
Height	2$\frac{1}{2}$ins (6.5cms)
Introduced	1989
Withdrawn	1996

BH10 Dusty Dogwood - Groom
Series	The Wedding
Story	*Summer Story*
Height	2$\frac{1}{2}$ins (6.5cms)
Introduced	1989
Withdrawn	1996

BH11 Dusty and Poppy - Bride and Groom
Series	The Wedding
Story	*Summer Story*
Height	2$\frac{1}{2}$ins (6.5cms)
Introduced	1990
Withdrawn	1995

BH12 Old Vole - Minister
Series	The Wedding
Story	*Summer Story*
Height	2$\frac{1}{4}$ins (5.5cms)
Introduced	1990
Withdrawn	1996

BH13 Wilfred - Pageboy
Series	The Wedding
Story	*Summer Story*
Height	2$\frac{1}{4}$ins (5.5cms)
Introduced	1990
Withdrawn	1996

BH14 Primrose - Bridesmaid
Series	The Wedding
Story	*Summer Story*
Height	2$\frac{1}{4}$ins (5.5cms)
Introduced	1990
Withdrawn	1996

BH15 Conker - Best Man
Series	The Wedding
Story	*Summer Story*
Height	2$\frac{1}{2}$ins (6.5cms)
Introduced	1990
Withdrawn	1996

BH16 Floral Arch
Series	The Wedding
Story	*Summer Story*
Height	5$\frac{1}{2}$ins (14cms)
Introduced	1990
Withdrawn	1995

BH17 Wedding Table and Canopy
Series	The Wedding
Story	*Summer Story*
Height	5$\frac{1}{4}$ins (13.5cms)
Introduced	1990
Withdrawn	1995

BH27 Mr Apple Proposing a Toast
Series	The Wedding
Story	*Summer Story*
Height	2$\frac{3}{4}$ins (7cms)
Introduced	1991
Withdrawn	1996

BH28 Lady Woodmouse Eating Cake
Series	The Wedding
Story	*Summer Story*
Height	2$\frac{3}{4}$ins (7cms)
Introduced	1991
Withdrawn	1996

MIDWINTER COLLECTION

BH18 Snowmouse
Series	Midwinter
Story	*Winter Story*
Height	2$\frac{1}{2}$ins (6.5cms)
Introduced	1990
Withdrawn	1993

BH19 Wilfred Reciting
Series	Midwinter
Story	*The Secret Staircase*
Height	2$\frac{1}{2}$ins (6.5cms)
Introduced	1990
Withdrawn	1993

BH20 Primrose Reciting
Series	Midwinter
Story	*The Secret Staircase*
Height	3ins (7.5cms)
Withdrawn	1993

BH21 Lady Woodmouse in a Chair
Series	Midwinter
Story	*The Secret Staircase*
Height	3ins (7.5cms)
Introduced	1990
Withdrawn	1993

BH22 Lord Woodmouse in a Chair
Series	Midwinter
Story	*The Secret Staircase*
Height	3ins (7.5cms)
Introduced	1990
Withdrawn	1993

BH23 Midwinter Tree
Series	Midwinter
Story	*The Secret Staircase*
Height	5$\frac{1}{2}$ins (14cms)
Introduced	1990
Withdrawn	1993

BH24 Midwinter Fireplace
Series	Midwinter
Story	*The Secret Staircase*
Height	4$\frac{3}{4}$ins (12cms)
Introduced	1990
Withdrawn	1993

BH37 Mrs Apple and Children
Series	Midwinter
Story	*The Secret Staircase*
Height	2$\frac{1}{2}$ins (6.5cms)
Introduced	1991
Withdrawn	1995

BH38 Basil Reclining
Series	Midwinter
Story	*The Secret Staircase*
Height	2$\frac{1}{2}$ins (6.5cms)
Introduced	1991
Withdrawn	1995

Top row: BH11 and BH16, BH17. Middle row: BH13, BH14, BH10, BH9. Bottom row: BH12, BH15, BH28, BH27.

Top row: BH19, BH20, BH22, BH21. Middle row: BH24, BH23. Bottom row: BH38, BH18, BH37.

NURSERY COLLECTION

Top row: BH32, BH34, BH29. Middle row: BH31, BH30, BH35. Bottom row: BH36, BH40, BH39, BH33.

NURSERY COLLECTION

BH29 Lady Woodmouse and Primrose
Series | Nursery
Story | *Autumn Story*
Height | 2³/₄ins (7cms)
Introduced | 1991
Withdrawn | 1994

BH30 Teasel
Series | Nursery
Story | *Winter Story*
Height | 2¹/₂ins (6.5cms)
Introduced | 1991
Withdrawn | 1996

BH31 Wilfred Jigging
Series | Nursery
Story | *Spring Story*
Height | 2¹/₂ins (6.5cms)
Introduced | 1991
Withdrawn | 1996

BH32 Clover and Catkin
Series | Nursery
Story | *Winter Story*
Height | 2¹/₂ins (6.5cms)
Introduced | 1991
Withdrawn | 1995

BH33 Dressing Table
Series | Nursery
Story | *Summer Story*
Height | 2³/₄ins (7cms)
Introduced | 1991
Withdrawn | 1995

BH34 The Canopy Bed
Series | Nursery
Story | *Autumn Story*
Height | 6ins (15cms)
Introduced | 1991
Withdrawn | 1995

BH35 The Bunk Beds
Series | Nursery
Story | *Winter Story*
Height | 4¹/₄ins (10.5cms)
Introduced | 1991
Withdrawn | 1995

BH36 The Toy Chest
Series | Nursery
Story | *The Secret Staircase*
Height | 2¹/₂ins (6.5cms)
Introduced | 1991
Withdrawn | 1995

BH39 Wilfred - Teddy Mouse
Series | Nursery
Story | *Winter Story*
Height | 2¹/₂ins (6.5cms)
Introduced | 1992
Withdrawn | 1996

BH40 Primrose - Teddy Mouse
Series | Nursery
Story | Not featured in these clothes
Height | 2¹/₄ins (5.5cms)
Introduced | 1992
Withdrawn | 1996

BH41-49 Not produced

MUSICALS

BH50-53
The musicals were first made with wooden feet and then with a metal revolving base.

BH50 Wilfred (Spring)
Series | Musicals
Story | *Spring Story*
Height | 3¹/₂ins (9cms)
Introduced | 1990
Withdrawn | 1995

The music played is *Hickory Dickory Dock* (with wooden feet) and *Deck the Halls* (with revolving base).

BH51 Primrose (Autumn)
Series | Musicals
Story | *Autumn Story*
Height | 3¹/₂ins (9cms)
Introduced | 1990
Withdrawn | 1995

The music played is *Mozart Minuet* (with wooden feet) and *Autumn Leaves* (with revolving base).

BH52 Poppy Eyebright (Summer)
Series | Musicals
Story | *Summer Story*
Height | 4ins (10cms)
Introduced | 1990
Withdrawn | 1995
The music played is *Mozart Minuet* (with revolving base).

BH53 Mrs Apple (Winter)
Series | Musicals
Story | *Spring Story*
Height | 4ins (10cms)
Introduced | 1990
Withdrawn | 1995
The music played is *Deck the Halls* (with wooden feet) and *Autumn Leaves* (with revolving base).

BH54-59 Not issued

Musicals: BH53, BH50, BH51, BH52.

THE PICNIC COLLECTION

Top row: BH66, BH61, BH66 (red). Middle row: BH67, BH64, BH63. Bottom row: BH62, BH60, BH65.

THE PICNIC COLLECTION

BH60 The Picnic Blanket
Series   The Picnic
Story   *Spring Story*
Height   1¹/₂ins (4cms)
Introduced   1993
Withdrawn   1999

BH61 Mr Toadflax
Series   The Picnic
Story   *Spring Story*
Height   2³/₄ins (7cms)
Introduced   1993
Withdrawn   1995

BH62 Mrs Toadflax and Hamper
Series   The Picnic
Story   *Spring Story*
Height   2¹/₂ins (6.5cms)
Introduced   1993
Withdrawn   1995

BH63 Wilfred with Toys
Series   The Picnic
Story   *Spring Story*
Height   2ins (5cms)
Introduced   1993
Withdrawn   1995

BH64 Basil with Basket
Series   The Picnic
Story   *Spring Story*
Height   2¹/₂ins (6.5cms)
Introduced   1993
Withdrawn   1995

BH65 Mrs Apple and Wilfred
Series   The Picnic
Story   *Spring Story*
Height   2³/₄ins (7cms)
Introduced   1993
Withdrawn   1995

POPPY'S BABIES COLLECTION

Top row: BH71, BH73, BH75. Bottom row: BH74, BH72, BH70.

BH66 Teasel and Clover
Series   The Picnic
Story   *Spring Story*
Height   2¹/₂ins (6.5cms)
Introduced   1993
Withdrawn   1995
A few figures were made with Teasel wearing a red striped jumper instead of the standard blue stripes. They are very rare.

BH67 Lord and Lady Woodmouse Resting
Series   The Picnic
Story   *Spring Story*
Height   2¹/₄ins (5.5cms)
Introduced   1993
Withdrawn   1995

BH68-69 Not produced

POPPY'S BABIES

BH70 Poppy and Babies
Series   Poppy's Babies
Story   *Poppy's Babies*
Height   2³/₄ins (7cms)
Introduced   1996
Withdrawn   1997

BH71 Lady Woodmouse Looking in Cradle
Series   Poppy's Babies
Story   *Poppy's Babies*
Height   2¹/₂ins (6.5cms)
Introduced   1996
Withdrawn   1997

BH72 Poppy Asleep in Chair
Series   Poppy's Babies
Story   *Poppy's Babies*
Height   2¹/₂ins (6.5cms)
Introduced   1996
Withdrawn   1997

BH73 Babies in Bath
Series   Poppy's Babies
Story   *Poppy's Babies*
Height   2ins (5cms)
Introduced   1996
Withdrawn   1997

BH74 Poppy Packing Nightclothes
Series   Poppy's Babies
Story   *Poppy's Babies*
Height   2³/₄ins (7cms)
Introduced   1996
Withdrawn   1997

BH75 Dusty Pushing Pram
Series   Poppy's Babies
Story   *Poppy's Babies*
Height   3¹/₄ins (8cms)
Introduced   1996
Withdrawn   1997

BH76-99 Not produced

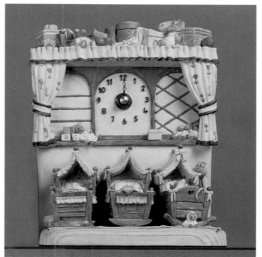

Top, BH101, bottom, BH100.

Top, BH102, bottom, BH105.

BH100 The Store Stump Clock
Series   Clocks
Story   *Spring Story*
Height   8¹/₄ins (21cms)
Introduced   1991
Withdrawn   1996

BH101 Nursery Clock
Series   Clocks
Story   *Autumn Story*
Height   8¹/₄ins (21cms)
Introduced   1992
Withdrawn   1996

BH102 Poppy's Babies Clock
Series   Clocks
Story   *Poppy's Babies*
Height   6³/₄ins (17cms)
Introduced   1996
Withdrawn   1997

BH103-104 Not produced

BH105 Harvest Mice
Series   Cameos
Story   *Autumn Story*
Height   4¹/₄ins (10.5cms)
Introduced   1991
Withdrawn   1994

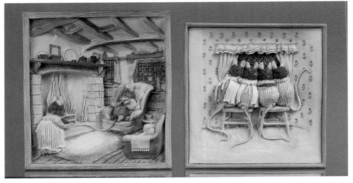

BH106, BH107

BHA4, BHA1

BHA2, BHA3

BHA5

BHMB01

BH106 Supper by the Fire
Series	Cameos
Story	*Winter Story*
Height	4¹/₂ins (11.5cms)
Introduced	1991
Withdrawn	1994

BH107 Snowy Window
Series	Cameos
Story	*Winter Story*
Height	4¹/₄ins (10.5cms)
Introduced	1991
Withdrawn	1994

The following **BHA, BHM, BHW** and **BHF** numbers were produced in China.

BHA1 Wilfred Flies a Kite
Series	Picture Frames
Story	Adapted from illustration, *Sea Story*
Height	6ins (15cms)
Introduced	1994
Withdrawn	1996

BHA2 Shrimp on the Sandcastle
Series	Picture Frames
Story	*Sea Story*
Height	5¹/₂ins (14cms)
Introduced	1994
Withdrawn	1996

BHA3 Mr Apple at the Dresser
Series	Picture Frames
Story	*Spring Story*
Height	5¹/₂ins (14cms)
Introduced	1994
Withdrawn	1996

BHA4 Under the Bluebells
Series	Picture Frames
Story	*Spring Story*
Height	6ins (15cms)
Introduced	1994
Withdrawn	1996

BHA5 Primrose in the Cornfield
Series	Picture Frames
Story	*Autumn Story*
Height	7¹/₄ins (18.5cms)
Introduced	1994
Withdrawn	1996

Poppy and Babies bookends.

Summer Tableau 'The Wedding'.

BHMB01   Rose in Cradle Money Box

Series	Poppy's Babies
Story	*Poppies Babies*
Height	6ins (16cms)
Introduced	1996
Withdrawn	1997

BHW01   Mice in Bath Water Ball

Series	Poppy's Babies
Story	*Poppy's Babies*
Height	5¹/₄ins (13.5cms)
Introduced	1996
Withdrawn	1997

BHB01   Poppy and Babies Bookends

Series	Poppy's Babies
Story	*Poppies Babies*
Height	5ins (12.5cms)
Introduced	1996
Withdrawn	1997

BHF01   Buttercup Picture Frame (Pink)

Series	Poppy's Babies
Story	*Poppy's Babies*
Height	3³/₄ins (9.5cms)
Introduced	1996
Withdrawn	1997

BHF02   Pipkin Picture Frame (Blue)

Series	Poppy's Babies
Story	*Poppy's Babies*
Height	3³/₄ins (9.5cms)
Introduced	1996
Withdrawn	1997

Buttercup and Pipkin picture frames with Mice in Bath water ball.

Disp 1   The Kitchen Display

Height	6¹/₂ins (16.5cms)
Introduced	1990
Withdrawn	1992

Also made by Enesco, see page 70.

Disp 2   The Wedding Display

Height	6¹/₂ins (16.5cms)
Introduced	1990
Withdrawn	1992

Also made by Enesco, see page 70.

Disp 3   The Midwinter Display

Height	6¹/₂ins (16.5cms)
Introduced	1991
Withdrawn	1992

Disp 4   The Nursery Display

Height	6¹/₂ins (16.5cms)
Introduced	1991
Withdrawn	1992

Also made by Enesco, see page 70.

Summer Tableau 'The Wedding'

Series	Four Seasons
	Tableaux
Story	*Summer Story*
Height	6¹/₂ins (16.5cms)

Introduced 1999 in a limited edition of 999. This Tableau was commissioned by Wheelers of Loughborough and is the first in a proposed series of 12 designs. The *Winter, Spring* and *Autumn* Tableaux will be launched during 1999 and 2000 together with a special Millennium Tableau of *The Snow Ball.*

ENESCO

RESIN FIGURES

The Enesco resin figures were made in China and distributed in the USA. The pieces were all modelled by Richard Wawrzesta and are the same as the Border Fine Arts designs. The Enesco cold cast resin tends to have a waxy finish that distinguishes it from the Border Fine Arts resin body. The figure collection was launched in 1990 and withdrawn by 1994.

THE STORE STUMP KITCHEN COLLECTION

Introduced in 1990 and withdrawn by 1994

698938 Mrs Apple

698911 Lady Woodmouse

698113 Primrose

698881 Wilfred

698946 Mr Apple in Rocking Chair

613711 Mrs Crustybread

698962 The Dresser

698954 The Table

698970 The Fireplace

THE WEDDING COLLECTION

Introduced in 1990 and withdrawn by 1994

697745 Poppy Eyebright - Bride

697753 Dusty Dogwood - Groom

614378 Dusty and Poppy - Bride and Groom

614300 Old Vole - Minister

614327 Wilfred - Pageboy

The Store Stump Kitchen Collection.

The Wedding Collection.

Nursery Collection.

The Picnic Collection.

614335 Primrose - Bridesmaid

614319 Conker - Best Man

613703 Mr Apple Proposes a Toast

614351 The Wedding Table and Canopy

613681 Basil

613673 Lady Woodmouse and Cake

614343 Floral Arch

NURSERY COLLECTION
Introduced in 1991 and withdrawn by 1994

617989 Primrose and Lady Woodmouse

622400 Teasel

617970 Wilfred

620114 Clover and Catkin

617903 Dressing Table

617911 Canopy Bed

617938 Bunk Bed

617954 Toy Chest

THE PICNIC COLLECTION
Introduced in 1992 and withdrawn by 1994

626422 The Picnic Blanket

614742 Mr Toadflax

626473 Mrs Toadflax and Hamper

618667 Wilfred

626430 Basil

626465 Mrs Apple and Wilfred

626503 Teasel and Clover

626449 Lady and Lord Woodmouse

626600 The Store Stump Clock
Height   8½ins (21.5cms)
Introduced   1992
Withdrawn   1994

PLAQUES
Introduced in 1992 and withdrawn by 1994

626546 Snowy Window

626678 Harvest Mice

626554 Supper by the Fire

MUSICALS
JACK IN THE BOX
This series was distributed in the USA and the UK

408824 Spring (Wilfred)
Series   Jack in the Box
Height   10ins (25.5cms)
Introduced   1990
Withdrawn   1994
The music is *Hickory, Dickory, Dock*.

408832 Summer (Poppy)
Series   Jack in the Box
Height   10ins (25.5cms)
Introduced   1990
Withdrawn   1994
The music is *Mozart Minuet*.

408840 Autumn (Primrose)
Series   Jack in the Box
Height   10ins (25.5cms)
Introduced   1990
Withdrawn   1994
The music is *Autumn Leaves*.

408859 Winter (Mrs Apple)
Series   Jack in the Box
Height   10ins (25.5cms)
Introduced   1990
Withdrawn   1994
The music is *Deck the Halls*.

Snowy Window, Harvest Mice and Supper by the Fire.

Jack in the Box musicals.

FOUR SEASONS MUSIC BOXES

This series was distributed in the USA and the UK.

415715 Spring
Series	Music Boxes
Height	6ins (15cms)
Introduced	1990
Withdrawn	1994

415723 Summer
Series	Music Boxes
Height	6ins (15cms)
Introduced	1990
Withdrawn	1994

415731 Autumn
Series	Music Boxes
Height	6ins (15cms)
Introduced	1990
Withdrawn	1994

415758 Winter
Series	Music Boxes
Height	6ins (15cms)
Introduced	1990
Withdrawn	1994

FOUR SEASONS MUSICALS (not illustrated)

These musicals have wooden feet and were made in China. Similar versions were produced by Border Fine Arts, firstly with wooden feet and then with a metal revolving base. See page 64.

696765 Wilfred
Series	Musicals
Height	3¹/₂ins (8.5cms)
Introduced	1990
Withdrawn	1994

696773 Poppy Eyebright
Series	Musicals
Height	3¹/₂ins (8.5cms)
Introduced	1990
Withdrawn	1994

696781 Primrose
Series	Musicals
Height	3¹/₂ins (8.5cms)
Introduced	1990
Withdrawn	1994

696803 Mrs Apple
Series	Musicals
Height	3¹/₂ins (8.5cms)
Introduced	1990
Withdrawn	1994

The Snow Ball
Series	Musicals
Height	4¹/₂ins (11.5cms)

This piece does not feature in existing catalogues and so may not have gone into production. The music is *The Dance of the Sugar Plum Fairy*. This musical has a metal revolving base and was made in Taiwan.

Four Seasons music boxes.

Wilfred on Treasure Chest, The Snow Ball, Primrose on Treasure Chest musicals.

619701 The Wedding

Series	Musicals
Height	6¹/₂ins (16.5cms)
Introduced	1991
Withdrawn	1994

The music is Mendelssohn's *Wedding March*.

TREASURE CHEST MUSICALS

These musicals have wooden feet and were made in China.

626589 Wilfred on Treasure Chest

Series	Musicals
Height	4¹/₂ins (11.5cms)
Introduced	1992
Withdrawn	1994

The music is *I Whistle a Happy Tune*.

626570 Primrose on Treasure Chest

Series	Musicals
Height	4¹/₂ins (11.5cms)
Introduced	1992
Withdrawn	1994

The music is *My Favourite Things*.

Spring and Summer water balls.

WATER BALLS

The Four Seasons water balls incorporate resin figures and were produced in Taiwan. They were sold with a paper label with a copyright date for 1989. The Spring model was also impressed B.H. c J. B. 1990. They were distributed in the USA and the UK.

696811 Spring (Wilfred)

Series	Water Balls
Story	*Spring Story*
Height	5¹/₂ins (13.5cms)
Introduced	1990
Withdrawn	1994

696838 Summer (Poppy)

Series	Water Balls
Story	*Summer Story*
Height	5¹/₂ins (13.5cms)
Introduced	1990
Withdrawn	1994

The Wedding musical.

Autumn and Winter water balls.

Wilfred and Primrose Teddy Mouse water balls.

Mrs Toadflax and Basil water balls.

696846 Autumn (Primrose)

Series	Water Balls
Story	*Autumn Story*
Height	5¹/₂ins (13.5cms)
Introduced	1990
Withdrawn	1994

696854 Winter (Mrs Apple)

Series	Water Balls
Story	*Winter Story*
Height	5¹/₂ins (13.5cms)
Introduced	1990
Withdrawn	1994

626627 Wilfred Teddy Mouse

Series	Water Balls
Story	*Winter Story*
Height	5¹/₂ins (13.5cms)
Introduced	1992
Withdrawn	1994

626619 Primrose Teddy Mouse

Series	Water Balls
Story	Not featured in these clothes
Height	5¹/₂ins (13.5cms)
Introduced	1992
Withdrawn	1994

626635 Mrs Toadflax

Series	Water Balls
Story	*Spring Story*
Height	5¹/₂ins (13.5cms)
Introduced	1992
Withdrawn	1994

626643 Basil

Series	Water Balls
Story	*Spring Story*
Height	5¹/₂ins (13.5cms)
Introduced	1992
Withdrawn	1994

Primrose and Wilfred book ornaments.

Four Seasons Book Ornaments 613630

These resin tree ornaments were produced in Taiwan and are impressed on the spine of the book B.H. c J.B. 1989 E. There was also a paper label.

Wilfred

Series	Tree Ornaments
Story	*Spring Story*
Height	2¹/₂ins (6.5cms)
Introduced	1990
Withdrawn	1994

Poppy

Series	Tree Ornaments
Story	*Summer Story*
Height	2¹/₂ins (6.5cms)
Introduced	1990
Withdrawn	1994

(not illustrated)

Primrose

Series	Tree Ornaments
Story	*Autumn Story*
Height	2¹/₂ins (6.5cms)
Introduced	1990
Withdrawn	1994

Mrs Apple

Series	Tree Ornaments
Story	*Winter Story*
Height	2¹/₂ins (6.5cms)
Introduced	1990
Withdrawn	1994

(not illustrated)

Wilfred and Book promotional piece.

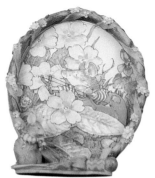

Wilfred picture frame.

Picture Frames 626511

The resin frames were made in China and sold with a paper label with copyright date for 1991.

Wilfred

Series	Picture Frames
Story	*Spring Story*
Height	4¹/₂ins (11.5cms)
Introduced	1992
Withdrawn	1994

Primrose

Series	Picture Frames
Story	*Autumn Story*
Height	4¹/₂ins (11.5cms)
Introduced	1992
Withdrawn	1994

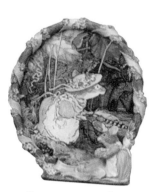

Primrose picture frame.

618268 Wilfred and Book promotional piece

Height	3¹/₄ins (8cms)
Introduced	1990
Withdrawn	1994

Four Seasons mugs.

Miniatures.

PORCELAIN PRODUCTS
APPLE ORNAMENTS

626538
These porcelain apple-shaped ornaments were sold in the US and the UK. Not illustrated.

Bedtime in Bunks
Story	*Winter Story*
Height	2¹/₂ins (6.5cms)
Introduced	1990
Withdrawn	1994

Mr Apple at Crabapple Cottage
Story	*Winter Story*
Height	2¹/₂ins (6.5cms)
Introduced	1990
Withdrawn	1994

The Snowmouse
Story	*Winter Story*
Height	2¹/₂ins (6.5cms)
Introduced	1990
Withdrawn	1994

FOUR SEASONS MUGS
The porcelain Spring, Summer, Autumn and Winter mugs were sold in the US.
Introduced   1991
Withdrawn   1994

MINIATURES 227218
The porcelain miniature teapot, bottle, beaker and vase were sold in the US and in the UK.
Introduced   1991
Withdrawn   1994

MELAMINE CHILD'S
DINNER SET 860425
This melamine five-piece set included a divided plate, bowl, mug, fork and spoon and was made in Taiwan. It was sold in the US and in the UK.
Introduced   1990
Withdrawn   1994

Child's Melamine dinner set.

Pewter figures: Primrose, Wilfred Toadflax, Poppy Eyebright, Dusty Dogwood, Mr Apple and Mrs Apple.

PEWTER FIGURES

The pewter figures are impressed E on the top of the base at the back and c J.B on the bottom of the base. They were all modelled by Richard Wawrzesta. They were distributed in the USA and in the UK.

698083 Poppy Eyebright
Series	Pewter
Story	*Summer Story*
Height	1³/₄ins (4.5cms)
Introduced	1990
Withdrawn	1994

698091 Dusty Dogwood
Series	Pewter
Story	*Summer Story*
Height	1³/₄ins (4.5cms)
Introduced	1990
Withdrawn	1994

698105 Wilfred Toadflax
Series	Pewter
Story	*Spring Story*
Height	1¹/₂ins (4cms)
Introduced	1990
Withdrawn	1994

698113 Primrose
Series	Pewter
Story	*Autumn Story*
Height	1³/₄ins (4.5cms)
Introduced	1990
Withdrawn	1994

698148 Mr Apple in his Rocking Chair
Series	Pewter
Story	*Spring Story*
Height	2¹/₄ins (5.5cms)
Introduced	1990
Withdrawn	1994

698121 Mrs Apple
Series	Pewter
Story	*Spring Story*
Height	1³/₄ins (4.5cms)
Introduced	1990
Withdrawn	1994

698156 Tree Trunk Home (in resin)
Story	*Spring Story*
Height	7³/₄ins (19.5cms)
Introduced	1990
Withdrawn	1994

Tree Trunk home for pewter figures.

Four Seasons Tree Stump thimbles: Wilfred, Primrose, Mrs Apple.

Four Seasons Tree Stump thimble, Poppy.

MINI PEWTER FIGURES
696870/ 620106
The pewter subjects were also available in a smaller size, 1¼ins high. They were distributed in the US and in the UK. Not illustrated.

Poppy Eyebright
Series	Mini Pewter
Story	*Summer Story*
Height	1¼ins (3.5cms)
Introduced	1990
Withdrawn	1994

Dusty Dogwood
Series	Mini Pewter
Story	*Summer Story*
Height	1¼ins (3.5cms)
Introduced	1990
Withdrawn	1994

Wilfred Toadflax
Series	Mini Pewter
Story	*Spring Story*
Height	1¼ins (3.5cms)
Introduced	1990
Withdrawn	1994

Mr Apple in his Rocking Chair
Series	Mini Pewter
Story	*Spring Story*
Height	1¼ins (3.5cms)
Introduced	1990
Withdrawn	1994

Mrs Apple
Series	Mini Pewter
Story	*Spring Story*
Height	1¼ins (3.5cms)
Introduced	1990
Withdrawn	1994

Clover
Series	Mini Pewter
Story	*Winter Story*
Height	1¼ins (3.5cms)
Introduced	1990
Withdrawn	1994

Catkin
Series	Mini Pewter
Story	*Winter Story*
Height	1¼ins (3.5cms)
Introduced	1990
Withdrawn	1994

Primrose
Series	Mini Pewter
Story	*Autumn Story*
Height	1¼ins (3.5cms)
Introduced	1990
Withdrawn	1994

Wilfred
Series	Mini Pewter
Story	*Spring Story*
Height	1¼ins (3.5cms)
Introduced	1990
Withdrawn	1994

THIMBLES
The pewter thimbles were all modelled by Richard Wawrzesta.

FOUR SEASONS TREE STUMP THIMBLES 696862
These thimbles are impressed B.H. c J.B. date year (e.g. 1989) E. They were distributed in the USA and in the UK.

Wilfred

Series	Tree Stump Thimbles
Story	*Spring Story*
Height	2ins (5cms)
Introduced	1990
Withdrawn	1994

Poppy

Series	Tree Stump Thimbles
Story	*Summer Story*
Height	2ins (5cms)
Introduced	1990
Withdrawn	1994

Primrose

Series	Tree Stump Thimbles
Story	*Autumn Story*
Height	2ins (5cms)
Introduced	1990
Withdrawn	1994

Mrs Apple

Series	Tree Stump Thimbles
Story	*Winter Story*
Height	2ins (5cms)
Introduced	1990
Withdrawn	1994

NURSERY BASKET THIMBLES 618276

This set was produced in Taiwan and distributed in the US. The figures on the thimbles are impressed E and the paper label has a copyright date for 1990.

Clover

Series	Nursery Basket Thimbles
Story	*Winter Story*
Height	2¼ins (5.5cms)
Introduced	1991
Withdrawn	1994

Occasionally the wrong figure is attached to the thimble base in error. For example, Clover has been found on a Preserve Pot instead of the Nursery Basket.

Catkin

Series	Nursery Basket Thimbles
Story	*Winter Story*
Height	2¼ins (5.5cms)
Introduced	1991
Withdrawn	1994

Primrose

Series	Nursery Basket Thimbles
Story	*Autumn Story*
Height	2¼ins (5cms)
Introduced	1991
Withdrawn	1994

Wilfred

Series	Nursery Basket Thimbles
Story	*Spring Story*
Height	2¼ins (5.5cms)
Introduced	1991
Withdrawn	1994

Nursery Basket thimbles: top row, Clover, and Wilfred; bottom row, Primrose and Catkin.

The Picnic thimbles: Mr Toadflax, Basil, Mrs Apple and Poppy.

THE PICNIC THIMBLES

626538

This set was produced in China and distributed in the US. They are impressed E.BH c JB 1991.

Mr Toadflax

Series	The Picnic Thimbles
Story	*Spring Story*
Height	2¹/₄ins (5.5cms)
Introduced	1992
Withdrawn	1994

Mrs Apple

Series	The Picnic Thimbles
Story	*Spring Story*
Height	2¹/₄ins (5.5cms)
Introduced	1991
Withdrawn	1994

Basil with Bottle

Series	The Picnic Thimbles
Story	*Summer Story*
Height	2¹/₄ins (5.5cms)
Introduced	1992
Withdrawn	1994

Poppy with Dairy Pails

Series	The Picnic Thimbles
Story	*Summer Story*
Height	2¹/₄ins (5.5cms)
Introduced	1992
Withdrawn	1994

TREASURE CHESTS

The resin treasure chests decorated with pewter figures were made in China and sold with a paper label with a copyright date for 1990.

618357 Wilfred

Series	Treasure Chests
Story	*The Secret Staircase*
Height	2¹/₄ins (5.5cms)
Introduced	1991
Withdrawn	1994

618365 Primrose

Series	Treasure Chests
Story	*The Secret Staircase*
Height	2¹/₄ins (5.5cms)
Introduced	1991
Withdrawn	1994

Primrose and Wilfred treasure chests.

MISCELLANEOUS
**651044 Miniature Wooden
Shadow Box**
Introduced 1991
Withdrawn 1992
(not illustrated)

651052 Miniature Accessories
Introduced 1991
Withdrawn 1992
(not illustrated)

569615 Set of three cake tins
Introduced 1990
Withdrawn 1994
These tins were made in Hong
Kong

**569577 Hexagonal tin with pot
pourri**
Introduced 1990
Withdrawn 1994
This tin was made in Hong Kong

**569585 Tin with handle and
acorn soap**
Introduced 1990
Withdrawn 1994

**569593 Lunch tin with two
handles**
Introduced 1990
Withdrawn 1994
(not illustrated)

581291 Set of four round tins
Introduced 1990
Withdrawn 1994

569569 Canister
Introduced 1990
Withdrawn 1994
(not illustrated)

Selection of tins.

Set of four round tins.

CRUMMLES

Enamel boxes were very fashionable in Georgian England and were given as love tokens or souvenirs to be used for all manner of personal effects from patches to snuff. The English became the acknowledged experts in the art of enamelling on copper, following the invention of transfer printing in the mid-eighteenth century, but this specialist craft virtually died out in the wake of the industrial revolution. After considerable research, the technique was revived in 1970 and, a few years later, John Aris founded Crummles and Company to cater for this new collecting interest.

As well as traditional designs, such as floral motifs, John Aris decided to introduce enamel boxes featuring characters from children's stories. The tales of Beatrix Potter provided the inspiration for his first collection in 1978 and this was followed by other classics such as *Alice in Wonderland, Paddington Bear* and *Winnie the Pooh*. The licence to reproduce Brambly Hedge characters was granted in 1983 and, during the next few years, Crummles introduced a series of round and oval boxes in various sizes as well as an enamel picture frame and a napkin ring. This delightful collection continued until 1995 when the company changed hands. Under the auspices of Country Artists, their new owners, Crummles have recently produced a new series of Brambly Hedge boxes especially for Lawleys by Post, the well-known mail order company for china and collectables.

Emma Potten is the current in-house designer at Crummles and she has the responsibility of translating Jill Barklem's book illustrations into delicate outline drawings suitable for the transfer printing process. She produced the detailed artwork for the Merry Midwinter's Eve box, which is the latest to be launched by Lawleys.

Crummles produce all their enamel boxes in Poole, Dorset, using manufacturing processes that have changed very little since the eighteenth century. First of all, the box is

Crummles promotional leaflet.

shaped from a thin sheet of pure copper and layers of enamel are fired on repeatedly until a fine glazed finish is perfected. Next, the outline transfer is applied to the enamel and fired into the surface. The artists then paint the boxes by hand, using specially mixed enamel colours, which are applied and fired many times to achieve a rich, glowing effect. Finally, the bezel and hinge are made from brass, silver-soldered and hand-finished. Crummles make all their own components, the only enamel box company to do so, and as a result their boxes have a very distinctive and satisfying click when they are closed.

Twentieth-century enamel boxes are now very collectable around the world and Crummles, with their outstanding reputation for children's characters, is one of the leading names in the collectable market. There is a thriving secondary market for their discontinued designs and their Brambly Hedge designs are particularly sought after.

Crummles catalogue showing the large Four Seasons boxes and *The Wedding* medium box.

Measuring the enamel ingredients.

Painting the design.

Coating the box with enamel and firing the enamel boxes.

L770 Spring (Wilfred)
Series   Large round boxes
Story   *Spring Story*
Height   2¼ins (5.5cms)
Introduced 1983
Withdrawn   1995

L771 Summer (Dusty and Poppy) (see illustration on p82)
Series   Large round boxes
Story   *Summer Story*
Height   2¼ins (5.5cms)
Introduced 1983
Withdrawn   1995

L772 Autumn (Primrose) (see illustration on p82)
Series   Large round boxes
Story   *Autumn Story*
Height   2¼ins (5.5cms)
Introduced 1983
Withdrawn   1995

L773 Winter (Mr Apple)
Series   Large round boxes
Story   *Winter Story*
Height   2¼ins (5.5cms)
Introduced 1983
Withdrawn   1995

M774 Mrs Apple and her Pot of Tea (see illustration on p82)
Series   Medium round boxes
Story   *Spring Story*
Height   1¾ins (4.5cms)
Introduced 1983
Withdrawn   1985

M775 The Wedding
Series   Medium round boxes
Story   *Summer Story*
Height   1¾ins (4.5cms)
Introduced 1983
Withdrawn   1995

M776 Dusty Miller with his Flour Sacks (see illustration on p82)
Series   Medium round boxes
Story   *Summer Story*
Height   1¾ins (4.5cms)
Introduced 1983
Withdrawn   1985

M777 Poppy at her Cooking (see illustration on p82)
Series   Medium round boxes
Story   *Summer Story*
Height   1¾ins (4.5cms)
Introduced 1983
Withdrawn   1985

M778 Four Small Mice
Series   Medium round boxes
Story   *Winter Story*
Height   1¾ins (4.5cms)
Introduced 1983
Withdrawn   1995

M779 Wilfred by the Fire at The Store Stump
Series   Medium round boxes
Story   *Spring Story*
Height   1¾ins (4.5cms)
Introduced 1983
Withdrawn   1985

X780 Spring Flowers
Series   Tiny round boxes
Story   *Spring Story*
Height   ½in (2cms)
Introduced 1983
Withdrawn   1995

X781 Summer Bouquet
Series   Tiny round boxes
Story   *Summer Story*
Height   ½in (2cms)
Introduced 1983
Withdrawn   1995

X782 Autumn Basket
Series   Tiny round boxes
Story   *Autumn Story*
Height   ½in (2cms)
Introduced 1983
Withdrawn   1995

X783 Winter Snow Mouse
Series   Tiny round boxes
Story   *Winter Story*
Height   ½in (2cms)
Introduced 1983
Withdrawn   1995

V284 Wilfred and Toys
Series   Medium oval boxes
Story   *Spring Story*
Height   1¾ins (4.5cms)
Introduced 1983
Withdrawn   1995

V285 Clover Toasting Bread
Series   Medium oval boxes
Story   *Winter Story*
Height   1¾ins (4.5cms)
Introduced 1983
Withdrawn   1995

From top to bottom, left to right: The Wedding, Wilfred and Toys, Clover Toasting Bread, The Palace Kitchen, Four Small Mice, Midwinter's Eve, Spring (Wilfred), Winter (Mr Apple), napkin ring, Summer Bouquet, picture frame, Winter Snow Mouse, Spring Flowers, Autumn Basket, Spring, Summer, Autumn and Winter (Lawleys by Post).

The Palace Kitchen

Series	Medium oval boxes
Story	*The Secret Staircase*
Height	1³/₄ins (4.5cms)
Introduced	1989
Withdrawn	1995

Spring (Wilfred Toadflax celebrates his birthday)

Series	Medium round boxes
Story	*Spring Story*
Height	1³/₄ins (4.5cms)
Introduced	1997
Withdrawn	1998

This design features a Royal Doulton backstamp and was commissioned by Lawleys by Post.

Summer (Poppy Eyebright and Dusty Dogwood announce their engagement)

Series	Medium round boxes
Story	*Summer Story*
Height	1³/₄ins (4.5cms)
Introduced	1997
Withdrawn	1998

This design features a Royal Doulton backstamp and was commissioned by Lawleys by Post.

Autumn (Primrose Woodmouse is lost in Chestnut Woods)

Series	Medium round boxes
Story	*Autumn Story*
Height	1³/₄ins (4.5cms)
Introduced	1997
Withdrawn	1998

This design features a Royal Doulton backstamp and was commissioned by Lawleys by Post.

Winter (Mr Apple at home in Crabtree Cottage)

Series	Medium round boxes
Story	*Winter Story*
Height	1³/₄ins (4.5cms)
Introduced	1997
Withdrawn	1998

This design features a Royal Doulton backstamp and was commissioned by Lawleys by Post.

Merry Midwinter's Eve

Series	Medium round boxes
Story	*Winter Story*
Height	1³/₄ins (4.5cms)
Introduced	1997 - Still current

This design features a Royal Doulton backstamp and was commissioned by Lawleys by Post.

Spring Napkin ring

Story	*Spring Story*
Height	1¹/₄ins (3.5cms)
Introduced	1987
Withdrawn	1995

Picture Frame

Story	*Summer Story*
Height	4ins (10cms)
Introduced	1987
Withdrawn	1995

Artwork for The Palace Kitchen oval box.

HANTEL VICTORIAN MINIATURES

Hantel Ltd. was established as a small family business in 1973 to produce a varied range of metal products. Initially based in Warwick, their early commissions included animal models in silver, bronze and pewter followed by a range of porcelain and silver jewellery. During the late 1970s, they worked very closely with the Royal Doulton group producing bronze accessories for a range of china figures. However, the speciality of the company dates from 1980 when their founder, Frances Wilson, began making miniature pewter figures with jointed limbs and applied colour to her models for the first time. These important innovations coincided with the company's move to a new location near Inverness in the Highlands of Scotland and local painters and craftsmen were trained to produce these tiny pieces. Originally the jointed miniatures, modelled on the scale of 1:12, were intended for the doll's house market but they soon began to attract a wider audience.

Frances Wilson, who created all the Hantel miniatures, trained as a sculptor at Coventry and Birmingham art schools before teaching art for a number of years. She was always fascinated with the world of miniatures and she soon began to combine her artistic skills with her love of nineteenth-century children's literature. Fairy tales and nursery rhymes inspired new Hantel collections such as Cinderella and The Owl and the Pussycat whilst the Alphabet and Punch and Judy collections were derived from Victorian toys and pastimes.

From traditional Victorian subjects, Frances expanded her horizons to include contemporary licensed characters, such as Kitty Cucumber created by Jim and Mary Lillemoe of California, and Steiff teddy bears. She has long been a fan of Jill Barklem's Brambly Hedge stories, having purchased the Four Seasons books shortly after they were published in the early 1980s. However, it was not until many years later that she saw a Copyrights feature about Brambly Hedge and approached them for more information. She was thrilled when she secured a licence in 1997 to reproduce the mice as pewter miniatures and started work on the prototypes without delay. The Spring Story collection was launched in 1998 and Frances then began working on Winter Story, featuring the four Toadflax children and Lord and Lady Woodmouse at the Snow Ball.

The tiny scale of the Hantel miniatures seems particularly appropriate for the Lilliputian world of Brambly Hedge. The mice characters measure just three-and-a-half centimetres and the various picnic accessories less than two centimetres. Jill Barklem was delighted with the intricate details achieved on these minute pieces, from the icing on Wilfred's birthday cake to the blue and white strips on the Cornish ware pudding bowl, one of her favourite kitchen patterns. Such marvellous detail is possible because of the modern rubber moulding methods used for pewter casting.

Frances Wilson at work.

Frances Wilson researched each new subject thoroughly before picking up her modelling tools. She always enjoyed working in clay and when producing the original models for her pewter miniatures, she used a special type known as Chevant clay, which is particularly stable and retains all the tiny details. A master craftsman would make rubber moulds from her clay original and then produce a pewter prototype, which was returned to Frances for more detailing. When she was satisfied with the finished effect, working moulds were made from the prototype so that the production models could be cast in molten pewter. Then the skilled painters set to work hand-decorating the tiny figures in specially formulated non-toxic colours. In total a new model could take up to three months to develop before the complex production process began and all the new Brambly Hedge designs also had to be approved by Jill Barklem and Copyrights.

From their home in the Highlands, the Hantel miniatures travelled far and wide and interest escalated in the 1990s with new collectors in the USA, Japan, Australia and Europe as well as the UK. A Collectors Society was formed in 1992 with exclusive limited edition offers and this served as a forum to keep members in touch with the growing secondary market for Hantel miniatures. Some of the earliest Frances Wilson models, such as the pewter parrot cage made between 1980 and 1982, now change hands for thousands of pounds. The enthusiasm of collectors also prompted the publication of a booklet listing all the Hantel models ever made, together with their production dates and edition sizes.

In 1998, Hantel celebrated their Silver Jubilee and a new showroom and administrative office were opened at Malvern in Worcestershire. The miniatures continued to be produced and decorated in the Highlands although Frances Wilson moved her studio back to her roots near the Malvern Hills, where she was joined by her daughter Rachel and son-in-law, Dean.

Sadly, Hantel ceased trading in March 1999 due to financial difficulties and prices of their miniatures have risen dramatically in the market-place. The Brambly Hedge *Spring* collection has become particularly desirable due to its short production period and it is a great shame that the *Winter* models did not come to fruition. Frances Wilson and her team at Hantel will be sorely missed but collectors will always delight in the magical miniature world that they created.

Spring Collection.

HANTEL PEWTER MINIATURES

The licence was issued in June 1997 and the *Spring Story* collection was launched in 1998. All the Hantel miniatures are modelled by Frances Wilson.

BH01 Wilfred
Story	*Spring Story*
Height	1in (3cms)
Introduced	1998
Withdrawn	1999

BH02 Mr Toadflax
Story	*Spring Story*
Height	1¼ins (3.5cms)
Introduced	1998
Withdrawn	1999

BH03 Mrs Toadflax
Story	*Spring Story*
Height	1¼ins (3.5cms)
Introduced	1998
Withdrawn	1999

BH04 Mr Apple
Story	*Spring Story*
Height	1¼ins (3.5cms)
Introduced	1998
Withdrawn	1999

BH05 Mrs Apple
Story	*Spring Story*
Height	1¼ins (3.5cms)
Introduced	1998
Withdrawn	1999

BH06 Handcart
Story	*Spring Story*
Height	1¼ins (3.5cms)
Introduced	1998
Withdrawn	1999

Wilfred investigating the hamper.

BH07 Hamper Set
Story	*Spring Story*
Height	¾in (1.6cms)
Introduced	1998
Withdrawn	1999

BH08 Hamper only

BH09 Basket Set
Story	*Spring Story*
Height	¾in (1.6cms)
Introduced	1998
Withdrawn	1999

BH10 Basket only

BH11 Goblets and Bottle Set
Story	*Spring Story*
Height	¾in (1.6cms)
Introduced	1998
Withdrawn	1999

BH12 Set of Three Puddings
Story	*Spring Story*
Height	½in (1.2cms)
Introduced	1998
Withdrawn	1999

COLLECTORS PLATES
AND PLAQUES

Collecting limited edition plates is a very popular hobby with several million devotees worldwide. Its origins can be traced to 1895 when the Danish firm, Bing and Grondahl, introduced an annual Christmas plate in their traditional blue and white style. The idea took off and it became the first of a series that is still going strong today. Other European firms followed suit and thus began a vogue that spread over Scandinavia and Northern Europe. Throughout the twentieth century, successive waves of immigrants imported their hobby to the United States and a wider audience was alerted to the attractions of the various plate series. The modern collectors plate market developed in the 1950s, when price lists for past issues began to circulate, and more manufacturers on both sides of the Atlantic entered the field.

Nowadays, collectors plates can be limited in several different ways. The size of the edition can be pre-announced and in some cases each plate is numbered. Alternatively, production can be limited to the year of issue or a pre-announced firing period. The enthusiasm for collectors plates now supports several periodicals and major conventions are held annually in North America. At the heart of the market is the Bradford Exchange, which is the world's largest trading centre for limited edition plates with offices in the US, Canada, Australia and all over Europe, including the UK. Their analysts monitor market trends and review current values in their various publications, notably the Bradex which is a kind of 'Stock Exchange' index for plates. However, their primary function is to facilitate the buying and selling of collectors plates and to that end they also commission exclusive designs from leading artists and manufacturers.

In 1994, the Bradford Exchange commissioned A Visit to Brambly Hedge, featuring four episodes from the Spring, Summer, Autumn and Winter stories. These oval-shaped designs were modelled in high relief and might be more accurately described as plaques. Richard Wawrzesta of Border Fine Arts was consulted on the modelling of this delightful series and the resin reliefs were manufactured in the Far East. This particular collection was limited by offer period and the edition closed on 15th August 1995.

Collectors plaques are also the speciality of the Lakeland Studios, located in Maryport at the edge of the Lake District. In 1998, they secured the licence to create a series of Brambly Hedge subjects in their well known three-dimensional format. Although framed for wall hanging, their relief sculptures are also supplied with a stand so that they can be displayed on a shelf. Their original Rural Heritage collection depicts the exteriors of famous British buildings, from cottages to castles, whilst their more recent Oval Room series features nostalgic interiors. As can be seen, their painstaking attention to detail made them the ideal choice to reproduce the habitats of the Brambly Hedge mice in three dimensions.

It was one of their sculptors, Joe Bailey, who first suggested the idea of interpreting Jill Barklem's illustrations for the Lakeland Studios range. Joe is an avid Brambly Hedge collector and so there was no shortage of inspiration around the walls of his own home on Biddulph Moor. It was obviously a labour of love for Joe to create the first six designs for the Brambly Hedge collection and he is looking forward to working on the next six later in 1999.

All the Lakeland Studios plaques are hand-cast in gypsum plaster and decorated with non-toxic paints by local artists. Collectors can watch painting and sculpting demonstrations at the company's new Visitor Centre in Maryport or, for those further afield, their Collectors Club is free of charge and provides details of events, new products and stockists.

Many collectors plates are promoted through advertisements in glossy magazines and colour supplements from national newspapers. Several UK companies specialise in this type of selling including the Danbury Mint of Chessington in Surrey. In 1998, they secured a licence to distribute a series of plates featuring scenes from Brambly Hedge and they chose the Wedgwood pottery to produce the designs. The advertisements featured four bone china plates, *Wilfred's Cake*, *The Harvest Mice*, *The Best Bedroom* and *Poppy's Babies* from a proposed series of twelve but unfortunately, due to technical difficulties, only *Wilfred's Cake* was produced. No doubt this sole Brambly Hedge plate from Danbury Mint will be sought after in the future.

BRADFORD EXCHANGE

Bradford Exchange was granted a licence to produce these relief modelled resin plates in 1994. Richard Wawrzesta was consulted on the design and they were produced in the Far East.

Winter Story

84-B10-081.1	**Summer Story**	84-B10-081.3	**Autumn Story**
Series	A Visit to Brambly Hedge	Series	A Visit to Brambly Hedge
Height	7¹/₂ins (19cms)	Height	7¹/₂ins (19cms)
Introduced	1994	Introduced	1994
Withdrawn	1995	Withdrawn	1995
84-B10-081.2	**Spring Story**	84-B10-081.4	**Winter Story**
Series	A Visit to Brambly Hedge	Series	A Visit to Brambly Hedge
Height	7¹/₂ins (19cms)	Height	7¹/₂ins (19cms)
Introduced	1994	Introduced	1994
Withdrawn	1995	Withdrawn	1995

Spring Story

Autumn Story

Summer Story

DANBURY MINT AND WEDGWOOD

Danbury Mint was granted a licence for a series of twelve collectors plates to be produced by Wedgwood and the first four designs were featured in the press during March 1998. Due to technical difficulties only the first plate was produced.

1 Wilfred's Cake (Icing the Cake)
Story	*Spring Story*
Height	8ins (20.5cms)
Introduced	1998 only

2 The Harvest Mice
Story	*Autumn Story*

3 The Best Bedroom
Story	*Spring Story*

4 Poppy's Babies
Story	*Poppy's Babies*

LAKELAND STUDIOS

Lakeland Studios secured a licence to produce relief modelled plaques in 1998. They were all designed by Joe Bailey and introduced in 1999. Each Brambly Hedge design is available in either a walnut or pine effect frame.

BH001 Primrose is Lost
Story	*Autumn Story*
Height	8ins (20.5cms)
Introduced	1999

BH002 First Taste
Story	*Sea Story*
Height	8ins (20.5cms)
Introduced	1999

BH003 Exploring the Nursery
Story	*The Secret Staircase*
Height	8ins (20.5cms)
Introduced	1999

BH004 The Engagement
Story	*Summer Story*
Height	8ins (20.5cms)
Introduced	1999

BH005 The Wedding
Story	*Summer Story*
Height	8ins (20.5cms)
Introduced	1999

BH006 Wilfred Visits the Store Stump
Story	*Spring Story*
Height	8ins (20.5cms)
Introduced	1999

Wilfred's Cake from Danbury Mint.

Danbury Mint advertisement showing other proposed designs.

Left, top to bottom: First Taste, Wilfred Visits the Store Stump, Primrose's Nest.
Above, top to bottom: The Wedding, Exploring the Nursery, The Engagement.

OTHER BRAMBLY HEDGE LICENSEES PAST AND PRESENT

Applewood's of Devon 1982-84
Cosmetics and soap

Apollo Sha's Jigsaw Puzzles 1992-C

Armstrong and Claydon 1992-94
Gift tin ware

Art Group 1991-96
Posters and prints without frames

Country Décor Wallcoverings 1997-C
Wallpaper and borders

Egmont Gifts 1991-94
Gift stationery

Euromark Pic 1995-96
Gift packed toiletries for Boots

Golden Bear 1985-98
Soft toys

Great American Puzzle Factory 1992-95
Jigsaws

Harvest Moon 1999-C
Needlecraft kits

John Ellam 1993-C
Framed decoupage pictures and kits

John Sands 1990-98
Cards, giftwrap and calendars

Lyric 1991-C
Notebooks and stationery for Japan

Mamelok Press 1998-C
Embossed scrapbook pictures

Manuscript 1987-1991
Framed prints

Marcel Shurman 1992
Stationery for USA

Magna Confectionery 1994-95
Money box with chocolates for Marks and Spencer

Pimpernell/Warnecke 1996-98
Four Seasons place mats and glassware

Reflex Marketing 1993-C
Postcards, greetings cards and stationery

Ripensa 1998-C
Danish Cookies in gift tins

Rose and Hubble 1997-C
Brambly Hedge fabric

Trax 1995-98
Notebooks and stationery for European market

Applewood's soap.

Selection of Brambly Hedge merchandise.

Applewood's lip gloss and scent.

Egmont Gifts stationery.

Copyrights brochure showing range of merchandise.

FURTHER READING

BRAMBLY HEDGE BOOKS

The Brambly Hedge books by Jill Barklem are all published by Collins. They are available in hardback, paperback and on audio cassette. Further information is available from Harper Collins Publishers Ltd., 77-85 Fulham Palace Road, Hammersmith, London W6 8JB

ORIGINAL STORIES

Spring Story first published 1980

Summer Story first published 1980

Autumn Story first published 1980

Winter Story first published 1980

The Secret Staircase first published 1983

The High Hills first published 1986

Sea Story first published 1990

Poppy's Babies first published 1994

Through the Hedgerow Pop Up Book 1983

TREASURIES AND COMPENDIUMS

The Brambly Hedge Pattern Book 1985

The Big Book of Brambly Hedge featuring poster size illustrations from the Four Seasons Books, first published 1981

The Four Seasons of Brambly Hedge including the *Spring, Summer, Autumn* and *Winter* Stories and a conversation with Jill Barklem, first published 1988

Tales from Brambly Hedge including the story of Brambly Hedge and *The Secret Staircase, The High Hills, Sea Story* and *Poppy's Babies*, first published 1997

COLLECTORS REFERENCE BOOKS

Cartoon Classics and other Character Figures by Louise Irvine, first published 1998

The Charlton Standard Catalogue of Royal Doulton & Beswick Storybook Figurines by Jean Dale with an introduction by Louise Irvine, first published in 1994

USEFUL ADDRESSES

Border Fine Arts
Townfoot
Langholm
Dumfries
Scotland DG13 0BR

Bradford Exchange
1 Castle Yard
Richmond
Surrey
TW10 6TF

Copyrights
Merchandise Agents for
  Writers and Artists
1 Ivory House
Plantation Wharf
Gartons Way
London SW11 3TN

Crummles & Co
3 Albion Close
Newtown Business Park
Poole
Dorset BH12 3LL

Danbury Mint
Cox Lane
Chessington
Surrey KT9 1SE

Lakeland Studios Ltd
Glasson Estate
Maryport
Cumbria
CA15 8NT

Royal Doulton
Minton House
London Road
Stoke-on-Trent
ST4 7QD